MW00615588

PLUM CRAZY

Drawings by Betty Fraser

PLUM CRAZY
A BOOK ABOUT BEACH PLUMS

ELIZABETH POST MIREL

 Clarkson N. Potter, Inc./Publisher   NEW YORK
DISTRIBUTED BY CROWN PUBLISHERS, INC.

Copyright © 1973 by Elizabeth Post Mirel.
All rights reserved.
No part of this publication may be reproduced, stored in a retrieval
system, or transmitted, in any form or by any means, electronic,
mechanical, photocopying, recording, or otherwise without prior
written permission from the publisher.
Inquiries should be addressed to Clarkson N. Potter, Inc.,
419 Park Avenue South, New York, N.Y. 10016
Library of Congress Catalog Card Number: 72-87336
ISBN: 0-517-50383-2
Printed in the United States of America
Published simultaneously in Canada by
General Publishing Company Limited
First edition.
Designed by Ruth Smerechniak

To Larry

Contents

Foreword

WHEN YOU THINK ABOUT BEACH PLUMS—IF YOU THINK about them at all—you associate them with jelly, but jelly is just the beginning. The little fruit lends itself to all sorts of preparations. Its story, although obscure, is fascinating.

Plum Crazy is a lighthearted miscellany. It is full of information about beach plums, gathered from published and unpublished sources, and from conversations with experts in various fields throughout the country. It includes some seventy recipes ranging from hors d'oeuvres to after-dinner drinks. The recipes are the result of three years of research and testing. Most are unusual, and nearly all are original. They are designed to use modern cooking equipment, to be simple to execute, and to make the most of the uncommonly tart flavor of beach plums. *Plum Crazy* also supplies suggestions for crafts based on beach plums. In addition to being fun, the projects demonstrate the remarkable versatility of the fruit.

Working with beach plums is like taking a vacation. If you keep a good supply at home, you can have a taste of summer any time of the year.

EPM

Acknowledgments

CONSTANCE CARTER OF THE LIBRARY OF CONGRESS, MURIEL Crossman of the Library of the Massachusetts Horticultural Society, Alan Fusonie of the National Agricultural Library, and Ann Graves Hunt of the Tea Lane Nursery, Chilmark, Massachusetts, ably guided my research. My children Helen (6), Paul (4), and Max (1) had valuable, unselfconscious reactions to the recipes. Susan Post and Anne Sigal edited the manuscript with unusual care and skill. My friends Elaine Freeman, Jackie Friedewald, and Brandy Jones scrutinized and tested the recipes. Many dinner guests sampled the preparations. Blooma Stark typed the manuscript with exceptional speed and accuracy. Marguerite Stevens lovingly cared for my children while I worked. My parents, Bill and Esther Post, willingly picked and provided for me for many years. My husband, Larry, gave me his sophisticated palate, sound judgment, and emotional support.

Life's a pudding full of plums;
Care's a canker that benumbs.
Wherefore waste our elocution
On impossible solution?
Life's a pleasant institution;
Let us take it as it comes.

—WILLIAM S. GILBERT
The Gondoliers

PART ONE

THE FRUIT

Being a Brief and True Account
of the History, Botany, and Nutrition
of the Beach Plum

In the Beginning

THE APPLE GOT THE CREDIT, BUT CHANCES ARE THE PLUM
was growing right beside it in the Garden of Eden. Plums
have been eaten for more than ten thousand years, since
Stone Age times when man depended on wild food for
nourishment.

Most of the plums we eat today trace their lineage to
ancient Middle Eastern ancestors. Plucked by Alexander
the Great in his fourth century B.C. Mediterranean cam-
paign, they were carried to Greece. Then, along with

Western history, they made their way to Italy, Europe, and America.

When the European plums immigrated to the New World, they were greeted at the shores by a native American species, *Prunus maritima*, the beach plum. Just as wild plums had supported early man in the Middle East, so they also were food for the first inhabitants of North America. The Indians used everything that was edible and attractive, and scholars are sure that beach plums were a part of their diet.* Beach plums may not match up to the finest European hybrids, but compared to acorns they make a tasty snack.

Early Written Records

The first writings on beach plums are contained in the diaries of early explorers. However, the men who discovered North America must have been better navigators than botanists. While their travel logs mention wild plums, the descriptions are usually unreliable. Historians have to assume that the wild plums found where beach plums now grow must actually have been beach plums.

The credit for first sighting the beach plum goes to

* William A. Ritchie, an archaeologist who specializes in Indian settlements, has conducted extensive investigations on Martha's Vineyard, where beach plums are abundant. The few remains of plant food he found were a handful of hickory nut shells, two charred kernels of corn, and one carbonized acorn. Not a single beach plum pit was discovered. Indirect evidence indicates, however, that beach plums were eaten by the early Indians, and the search for ancient vegetable remains continues.

Giovanni da Verrazano. In his 1524 explorations he discovered what had to be the beach plum growing along
the New York coast—but he mistakenly labeled it a dam-
son, a similar plum common in Europe.

John Brereton, a passenger on the English ship of Bar-
tholomew Gosnold, wrote in 1602 of the impressive
assemblage of wild plums on Martha's Vineyard. Henry
Hudson made a notation in 1609 of the abundant blue
plums at the mouth of the river named after him.

Casual observations of beach plums were made con-
tinually by settlers and travelers throughout the seven-
teenth and eighteenth centuries. Then the botanists, with
their penchant for description and classification, arrived
on the scene.

How the Beach Plum Got Its Name

Humphry Marshall, a farmer turned botanist, wrote the
first scientific description of *Prunus maritima* in 1785.
However, he was not recognized as the originator of the
species for over 100 years. Botanists thought F. A. J. von
Wangenheim named the beach plum in his 1781 treatise,
*Beschreibung einiger Nordamericanischen Holz- und
Buscharten.*

Von Wangenheim actually described the plant in 1787
—two years after Marshall—in a different text, *Beytrag
zur teutschen holzgerechten Forstwissenschaft, die An-
pflanzung Nordamericanischer Holzarten,* but botanists
confused the two long-titled books. Finally, in 1915,
William F. Wight, an American government scientist,

checked every page of the von Wangenheim books and exposed the mixup. Marshall was vindicated.*

Marshall's original description of *Prunus maritima*, the "Sea side Plumb," follows:

> *This grows naturally towards the sea coast, rising to the height of eight or ten feet, often leaning, and spreading into many branches. The leaves are oblong, rather smaller, and not so pointed as those of the common plumb; smooth and of a shining green on the upper side, but something lighter underneath, and slightly sawed on the edges. This is generally well filled with flowers, a few of which are succeeded by small, roundish fruit.†*

(It must have been a bad season. The size of the beach plum crop varies widely from year to year—a condition that has discouraged many attempts at commercialization.)

Domesticating the Wild Plant

The horticulturists followed on the heels of the botanists. In the early 1800s they made numerous efforts to cultivate beach plums. Several varieties are listed in the nur-

* Von Wangenheim was a Hessian officer fighting for the British in the Revolutionary War. While stationed on Long Island, he undoubtedly spent his off-duty hours gathering material for his field guides to American plants. He wrote them when he returned to Germany. Von Wangenheim also brought seeds home with him, and so has the distinction of being the first man to cultivate beach plums overseas. As a result of his work, and that of several others in later years, beach plums now grow in Europe and in Great Britain.

† Humphry Marshall, *Arbustum Americanum: The American Grove* (Facsimile of the 1785 edition) New York: Hafner, 1967, p. 112.

sery catalogs of the time. However, as forays into the West brought back larger and sweeter types of plums, domestication of *Prunus maritima* lapsed.

Then Luther Burbank became intrigued with the fruit at the end of the nineteenth century. The famous breeder of plants thought beach plums would make a good commercial crop because they are so hardy, so prolific, and bear fruit so late in the growing season. Burbank's brief affair with beach plums came to an unhappy end when his *Giant maritima* bore plums that were the size of grapefruits but turned out to be soggy.

In the early 1930s Ocean Spray Beach Plum Jelly was selling alongside Ocean Spray cranberry products, but the company apparently did not cultivate the plant. It abandoned the beach plum project after a few years because variations in the crop yield made it financially unviable.

Interest in beach plums revived in the 1940s when the economic rigors of World War II led Americans to investigate the possibilities of living off native crops. The only existing nutritional analysis of beach plums was done at this time, as was the work of George Graves, a Martha's Vineyard horticulturist devoted to gathering information about beach plums and to improving beach plum crop production. Although several named varieties can be purchased today, the cultivation of beach plums remains infrequent.

Cookery

While horticulturists might have been dubious about the value of cultivating beach plums, local populations have been quick to capitalize on their tart flavor. The early colonists ate the wild plums raw. A Pilgrim's 1621 letter to England described them as tasting "almost as good as a Damsen."* Wild plums were eaten along with dried berries for dessert at the first Thanksgiving dinner.

Colonial housewives made a variety of beach plum preserves for home consumption. Records indicate that, by

* Quoted in William A. Ritchie, *The Archaeology of Martha's Vineyard*, Garden City, N.Y.: The Natural History Press, 1969, p. 7.

the nineteenth century, beach plum jam, jelly, and juice were being produced for sale in local markets. These products are still made today by thousands of vacationers, summer residents, and year-round shore dwellers who find both the picking and the taste of the fruit irresistible.

A Beach Plum by Any Other Name

BEACH PLUMS HAVE KEPT BOTANISTS BUSY ON THE DUNES for the past two hundred years. Everything about the plant varies—distribution, size, shape, leaves, fruit, yield, flowers—and this capriciousness plays havoc with attempts at orderly classification.

Distribution

Botanists agree that beach plums grow along the Atlantic coast from Maine to Virginia, but some say they grow as far north as Canada and others that they reach as far south as the Carolinas. Several add that they are found around the Great Lakes, and a few mention the Gulf Coast.

The confusion has developed because the older botanical texts call the wild plums by many different, nonscientific names and often contain overlapping descriptions of their characteristics. This lack of clarity, coupled with the natural variability of the plant, makes accurate determination of the species difficult.*

* From a practical point of view, you can make anything in this book with any wild plums you can find. If they are growing along the northeast Atlantic coast, on the southern shores of Lake Michigan, and in sandy inland areas such as the New Jersey pine barrens, they are likely to be beach plums. To the far north, they may be Canada plums, to the Deep South, they may be Wild Goose plums, and to the Midwest, they may be Alleghany plums, but the name will not change the taste or alter the method of preparation.

Size and Shape

Some beach plum plants are tall and shapely; others are low and spreading. If you are used to seeing one form, you can hardly believe the other exists. Botanists once assigned the tall and low plants to two different species, the beach plum and the dwarf plum. Now they are considered varieties of the one species, *Prunus maritima*.

Leaves

The leaves of the beach plum are jagged around the edges, but some are more serrated than others. The leaves are elliptical, but some are more egg-shaped than others. The leaves are smooth, but some are hairy on the underside.

Fruit

The beach plum ripens from late August to early October. It can be as small as a pea or as large as a crabapple. The color of the ripe fruit ranges from red to purple to black, and even includes yellow. Take your pick.

Yield

Some years the beach plum crop is tremendous, and some years it is meager. One explanation for the discrepancy is that the size of the yield depends on atmospheric conditions at flowering time. If the weather is very cold, rainy, and windy, it may so hamper the work of the bees that the cross-pollination required for fruit production does not occur.

Another theory is that the beach plum does not get enough nitrogen in its sandy, wild environment. This element, essential for fruit production, may be used up each time the plant sets a good crop, and it may take the next few years to rebuild the supply. Some growers plant several varieties of beach plums so that the sparse yield of one type will be offset by the bumper crop of another.

Flowers

The one aspect of the beach plum that does not vary is the beauty of the bloom. The lacy flowers that appear in May or June charm gardeners and casual viewers alike. The flowers are so profuse that botanists have been able to plot the location of the blossoming plants from an airplane. The color of the flowers, however, often changes from white to light pink on older plants.

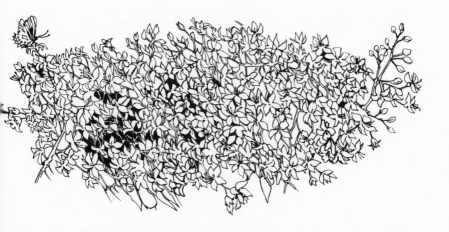

Good for You and Tasty Too

BEACH PLUMS, WITH ONLY 50 CALORIES TO THE CUP, ARE loaded with vitamin A, have a modicum of vitamin C, and contain traces of the B vitamins and protein. Their mineral content is five times as rich as that of their neighbor, the cranberry.

An analysis of the nutritional makeup of beach plums reveals the following values for 100 grams—about a cup—of the fruit:*

Water	87 percent
Food energy	50 calories
Protein	less than 1 percent
Fat	less than 1 percent
Carbohydrates	12 percent
Vitamin A	1000 international units
Vitamin C	(8 mg.)
Thiamine	trace
Riboflavin	trace
Niacin	(.5 mg.)
Vitamin B6	(.5 mg.)
Ash (minerals)	less than 1 percent
Potassium	(180 mg.)
Calcium	(20 mg.)
Phosphorus	(15 mg.)
Magnesium	(8 mg.)
Iron	(.5 mg.)
Sodium	(1 mg.)

* S. G. Davis and A. S. Levine, "Composition and Utilization of the Beach Plum," *The Fruit Products Journal* 21 (August 1942): 361–364. Values in parentheses are my estimates, based on several other studies of related species.

Medicinal Value

Old popular writings refer occasionally to the medicinal value of the beach plum. A colonial historian described the wild plum as being "very palatable to the sick."* The belief that the beach plum "is supposed to possess medicinal qualities" was noted by a nineteenth-century horticulturist.†

Modern scientific evidence of the healing properties of beach plums is, at best, indirect. Beach plums, like other plums, have a high pectin content. (This is why beach plum jam or jelly can be made by simply boiling the fruit

* Quoted in William F. Wight, *Native American Species of Prunus*, U.S. Department of Agriculture Bulletin 179, Washington, D.C.: U.S. Government Printing Office, April 1915, p. 4.

† *Ibid.*, p. 7. Both remarks refer to unspecified wild plums whose characteristics match those of beach plums.

or juice with sugar and water.) Pectin has recently come to the attention of medical researchers as a substance that reduces the level of cholesterol in the blood.

The effect appears to be undisputed, but the causes are not yet understood. One explanation is that pectin increases excretion and so prevents the absorption of cholesterol by the body. Another theory is that pectin somehow counteracts the body's production of cholesterol in the first place.

Pectin is also being examined as a weapon against bacteria and fungus, and for its role in preventing lead poisoning. Current medical literature includes studies of the minerals in Carpathian wild berries, the vitamins in black currants, and the medicinal substances in wild carrot seeds —but nothing on beach plums. Perhaps scientists ought to pay more attention to the little fruit. At the very least, the shore is a nice place to do research.

PART TWO

THE WORK

How to Pick,
Pack, Prepare, and Process
A Peck of Beach Plums

Where Are They?

WHETHER YOU ARE A NEW OR A LONG-TIME SHORE DWELLER, you may have overlooked beach plums. The modest plant seems to hide in the sand. In midsummer its tiny green immature fruits are barely noticeable. At the end of the summer the ripe, cherry-like crop hangs on the undersides of the branches, often dragging them into the sand with its weight. (These heavy limbs are harvester's prizes.)

Beach plums grow in the quiet, sunbaked valley created as the dunes dip down beyond the sea. There, close to the water table, the plants can sink their long taproots and take hold. The beach plum grows singly, in small clusters, or in dense thickets. Its dark, purplish bark is covered with light scars. The older growth may look weathered and gnarled, and it is often covered with interesting lichen.

Let a song sparrow guide you to the beach plum, for that is where it builds its nest. Bobwhites, downy woodpeckers, and flickers also live in beach plum thickets.

Other plants provide clues. Salt-spray roses, bayberries, and poison ivy like to grow where beach plums do. The bright red rose hips, the clusters of small gray berries, or the shiny trio of toxic green leaves are easily spotted.

You can dispense with natural history altogether and ask a neighbor to tell you the location of a choice beach plum thicket. If you have no neighbors to ask, try driving along side roads by the ocean, a bay, or an inlet in late August or early September. Watch carefully for the telltale signs of beach plums—a glimmer of burgundy fruit, a car pulled off in the sand. The occupants are probably out picking beach plums. Latch onto your bucket and follow their footprints.

Tips on Picking

When picking beach plums, the idea is to get a lot of fruit and nothing else. The following suggestions may be helpful.

1. Dress in long pants and a long-sleeved shirt to protect against poison ivy and brambles. It's better to be hot in the beginning than itchy or bloody afterward.

2. Douse yourself liberally with mosquito repellent. Some years the bugs are more abundant than the plums.

3. Bring a clean bucket for each picker and a good supply of plastic bags. They will fill up quickly.

4. Take children. Even three-year-olds are good pickers. Most beach plums are so tart that they go directly from hand to bag without the benefit of parental admonitions.

5. Pick firm fruit. Almost-ripe beach plums keep best. The very ripe ones, although they are the sweetest, tend to squish all over the bag. This makes sorting a messy job. Try nibbling on the ripe fruit as you move along the dunes.

6. Pick clean. Fruit harvested without leaves and stems can be stored as is.

Transportation

IF YOU JUST WANT TO GET THE BEACH PLUMS TO YOUR winter home, keep them in the refrigerator until you are ready to go. They take up a lot of space, but you should have a few empty shelves at the end of the season, anyway. The beach plums can sit comfortably in the refrigerator for about a week.

Load the bags of beach plums into the car with the rest of the luggage, but do not pack them on the roof. The heat might spoil them. Beach plums will last several days unrefrigerated—enough time to drive almost anywhere in this country.

Getting Ready for Winter

IF YOU DID A GOOD JOB OF PICKING, YOU CAN SIMPLY PUT your bags of beach plums right into the freezer. I like to pick quickly, so my bags always include a nasty amount of leaves, stems, and sand. I have to go over the beach plums carefully before storing them. This means stemming, rinsing, and thoroughly drying them. As I am doing this, I sort out the bruised and ripe beach plums and drop them into a large jar. They are the beginnings of a fine liqueur or brandy.

Freezing

Put the firm beach plums in plastic bags and place the bags in the freezer. If the beach plums have been wiped dry, they will not stick together and you can easily get whatever quantity you need at any time.

If your freezer space is limited and the whole supply cannot be frozen, process some beach plums right away. Do keep a corner of the freezer for at least one bag of the fresh fruit. Even if the beach plums spill every time you reach for the chopped parsley, you will want them for some of the recipes that require an uncooked product.

Beach plums will keep indefinitely in the freezer. I have had no trouble working with beach plums that were more than a year old. Beach plum products will keep for many months in the refrigerator if packed in clean containers.

Sterilizing

If beach plum products are going to be kept on the shelf, sterile packing is necessary. To do this, boil the jars, lids, and tongs for 15 minutes. Keeping the water simmering, take the jars one at a time, pour the hot beach plum product into them, and seal them immediately with paraffin or with self-sealing covers.

Introducing the
Basic Beach Plum Products

PICKING BEACH PLUMS IS SUCH A RELAXING WAY TO SPEND
even the dreariest of late summer days that it can hardly
be called a job. There is a tendency to harvest too many
beach plums, just for the pleasure of picking. You end up
with a freezer full of fruit or a shelf overstocked with
jelly. With a bit of attention to the following instructions,
however, you will be able to use them all and wish you
had picked more.

Beach plums can be processed in great batches or a bit
at a time. While it is convenient to have a supply of beach
plum products on hand so you can cook with them when-
ever you fancy, in most cases you can work along from
recipe to recipe, making just the small amount of the
product that is required.

The recipes that follow use beach plums in these forms:
whole, pitted, pulp, stew, jelly, sweetmeats, candies, and
shrub. Whole and pitted beach plums are the uncooked
fruit. They add an unusual taste to many fish, poultry,
and meat dishes, and are the basis of several fine beverages.
Pulp, beach plums ground into the tiniest of morsels, is
used mainly with meats and in sauces and desserts. Stew
is a simple-to-make preserve with a rich taste and chewy
consistency. It adds character to vegetables and baked
goods.

One simple procedure I devised while working with
beach plums makes jelly as well as sweetmeats or candies.
Jelly is fruit, sugar, and water boiled and then filtered

through coffee filter paper. Sweetmeats are pitted, and candies are whole beach plums. They are both by-products of the jelly-making process. The winelike taste of beach plum jelly is delicious in poultry and meat preparations as well as in sauces and desserts. Sweetmeats complement meat, vegetable, and baked dishes. While candies cannot be used in baking—unless you don't mind spitting out the pits—they are suitable for some simmered dishes, and they make a delectable snack.

Shrub is a thick syrup made with beach plums, vinegar, and sugar. It is best used to make fantastic cocktails, but it also adds a special flavor to soup and fish. (The word "shrub" comes from the Arabic *shurb*, a fruit drink. "Syrup" and "sherbet" are also derived from this root.) Shrub, an ancient preparation, was probably brought back to Europe by the Crusaders. In this country fruit shrubs were commonly prepared in colonial times. The zesty taste of beach plum shrub ought to encourage a revival of the practice.

Check the instructions to see how easy it is to make the basic beach plum products, and then read through the recipes to find out how they are used. Go ahead and make some jelly and sweetmeats. Gear yourself up and make a pot of stew. Cook something. If you have been wary of beach plums, the results will win you over.

PART THREE

THE BASIC
BEACH PLUM PRODUCTS

Without Which Nothing

A basic beach plum product—whole, pitted, pulp, stew, jelly, sweetmeats, candies, or shrub—will be required in each recipe. Instructions for preparing the products follow.

Whole Beach Plums

Even if you refuse to pit a single beach plum you can still make many remarkable foods and drinks.

1. Remove the specified quantity of beach plums from the freezer. (There are about fifty beach plums to the cup.) Rinse the beach plums quickly if they were not previously washed.

2. Use as is. The thawing fruit exudes juice that should not be lost or drained.

Pitted Beach Plums

Don't shy away from beach plums on the grounds that pitting is tedious. It takes only three minutes to pit one cup of beach plums, compared with two minutes to peel, core, and cut one apple—and pitting beach plums is much more satisfying.

Assembly Line Method

Several kinds of cherry stoners are available at kitchen supply shops and departments, and most are suitable for pitting beach plums. The best is a spring plunger. To use it, you place the beach plum on a supporting ring and press a narrow spike through it. This forces the pit out of the bottom of the fruit. (Commercial cherry packers use this technique on a larger, automated scale.)

1. Take about 4 cups of beach plums from the freezer. Place about 1 cup of the beach plums in a colander and run cold water over them. Pit the beach plums when they are half thawed.

2. While pitting one cup run the next cup under cold water, and so on. The beach plums should be pitted before they are fully thawed since the device does not work well on soggy fruit.

3. Use the pitted beach plums in a recipe or pack them in small plastic bags (½ cup in each bag) and return them to the freezer.

Jack Horner Method

This is the easiest way to hand-pit beach plums.

1. Run the frozen beach plums under cold water until they are thawed and soggy.

2. Pry them open with your thumbs, or cut them open with a knife, and pull out the pits. Watch out for squirting juice.

3. Use the pitted beach plums in a recipe or pack them in small plastic bags (½ cup in each bag) and return them to the freezer.

Frozen Fruit Method

A cleaner, but more time-consuming, way of pitting by hand requires working with totally frozen beach plums.

1. Remove the beach plums from the freezer in small batches. Cut the fruit away from the pit with a sharp knife.

2. Use the beach plum pieces in a recipe requiring pitted beach plums or pack them in small plastic bags (½ cup in each bag) and return them to the freezer.

A Note on Beach Plum Pits

Save the pits! It is essential to be frugal with beach plums. Your resources are limited. There is usually some fruit clinging to the pit after it has been extracted by any one of these methods. The pulpy pits can be frozen and used either by themselves or, preferably, as a supplement to the whole fruit. The pits can also be tied in all-purpose cloth (such as Handi-Wipes) or in cheesecloth and immersed in anything you are making with pitted fruit. The seed inside the pit has a lovely, light almond flavor that imparts added delicacy to the preparation.

Beach Plum Pulp

I have seen directions for making Beach Plum Pulp that require putting the fruit, pit and all, through a food mill. This is a ghastly experience. If you want to use a food mill, it is far less time consuming to pit the beach plums first and then mill the fruit. You can also use a blender.

Food Mill Method

1. Simmer 2 cups of pitted beach plums in ⅔ cup water for 30 minutes, or until they are soft. Force the fruit through a food mill or a coarse strainer.

2. Use the pulp in a recipe, or pack it in measured quantities and keep it in the freezer.

Makes about 1 cup.

Blender Method

1. Place 2 cups of pitted beach plums in the blender with ½ cup water. Blend at high speed until the skin pieces are barely visible. Add water by tablespoons, if necessary for blending.

2. Strain the pulp, if desired. (Blender beach plum pulp has the color and consistency of strawberry pulp. If you would strain strawberry pulp to remove the seeds, then strain beach plum pulp to eliminate the pieces of skin. I prefer the pulp unstrained.)

3. Use the pulp in a recipe, or pack it in measured quantities and keep it in the freezer.

Makes about 1½ cups unstrained and about 1 cup strained.

Beach Plum Stew

Beach Plum Stew is sometimes called a preserve, but "preserve" implies something sterile that sits on an unreachable shelf. Beach Plum Stew is too exciting for that name.

> 4 *cups pitted beach plums*
> 4 *cups sugar*
> 1⅓ *cups water*
> ½ *cup pulpy pits (optional)*

1. Place the beach plums, sugar, and water in a saucepan. If using the pits, tie them in all-purpose cloth (such as Handi-Wipes) or in cheesecloth, and immerse them in the liquid.

2. Bring the mixture to a boil and boil hard for 1 minute, stirring constantly. Reduce the heat and simmer for 30 minutes, or until the fruit is soft and the liquid is the consistency of thin syrup. Stir occasionally.

3. Remove the bundle of pits. Pour the stew into jars. Cover or seal and let cool. Use the stew in a recipe or save it for later. Keep in the refrigerator, or, if sterile-packed, on the shelf. (Beach Plum Stew will thicken as it cools. If it becomes too thick, stir in boiling water by tablespoons until the desired consistency is obtained. Cook the stew over lower heat next time.)

Makes about 5 cups.

Beach Plum Jelly

Before producing jelly, you must decide whether you want Natural Beach Plum Jelly, made with fruit, sugar, and water only, or Standard Beach Plum Jelly, made with fruit, sugar, water, and added pectin. The adherents of Natural Beach Plum Jelly claim that pectin is an unnecessary adulterant. The advocates of Standard Beach Plum Jelly state that making jelly without added pectin is risky. The following is some solid information on which you can base your decision.

Making Natural Beach Plum Jelly is a simple, easy-to-regulate process. It yields a full-bodied product that holds its flavor well. The method I have devised has the advantage of producing sweetmeats or candies as a by-product, so that nothing is wasted.

Preparing Standard Beach Plum Jelly requires extra sugar along with the added pectin. This combination detracts somewhat from the full flavor of the fruit, but it does keep the texture of the jelly consistent in storage over long periods of time. (My jelly is used so quickly that storage is not my main concern.) Standard Beach Plum Jelly starts with beach plum juice, and making juice is wasteful. It leaves a soggy mass of pulp and pits that can only be discarded.

Despite my bias in favor of Natural Beach Plum Jelly, I recognize that jelly made without added pectin occasionally refuses to jell. Superstitious cooks may blame this on the weather. Scientific-minded cooks may look to the properties of the particular batch of fruit, but are usually unaware of the full explanation.

The beach plum is a borderline fruit as far as jelling is concerned. The pH of beach plum juice is 3.3. If the juice were any more acid, it would not jell. The pectin present in beach plum juice is 0.09 percent. This is close to the lowest amount required for juice to jell.* Small natural variations in the acid and pectin levels may be just enough to thwart jelling.

Beach plums picked from plants that grow in light, sandy soil should have the right amounts of acid and pectin for jelling. Beach plums that grow in heavy soil, however, may have too rich an environment, and the fruit may take on extra tannin. Tannin, a compound deposited below the skin, is what gives beach plums their astringent taste. The added tannin increases the acidity of the fruit and throws the whole jelling ratio off balance.

Instead of watching the weather or examining the color of your fruit, note where you did your picking. Beach plums harvested in a sandy spot should give you no trouble. Beach plums picked in a swampy or woodsy area probably need added pectin to make jelly.

---

* Whole beach plums have a much higher pectin content than beach plum juice, so you should never have any difficulty making beach plum stew, butter, or jam. No study, however, has measured the amount of pectin present in the skin and pulp.

Natural Beach Plum Jelly

2 *cups pitted beach plums*
2 *cups sugar*
1 *cup water*
¼ *cup pulpy pits (optional)*

1. Place the beach plums, sugar, and water in a saucepan. (The ripest fruit yields the most juice, but the underripe fruit gives an especially tart flavor, so it is a good idea to use a combination.) If using the pits, tie them in all-purpose cloth (such as Handi-Wipes) or in cheesecloth and immerse them in the liquid.

2. Bring the mixture to a full boil and boil hard for 1 minute, stirring constantly. Reduce the heat and simmer for 45 minutes, or until the beach plums are saturated with sugar, and the liquid is the consistency of thin syrup. Stir occasionally.

3. Remove the bundle of pits. Pour the hot liquid into a coffee filter paper (such as Melitta or Chemex), supported

in a cone or funnel, and placed over a jar. Filter for 1 hour, or until most of the liquid has dripped out. If the original paper becomes clogged, and the liquid no longer drips out steadily, transfer the contents of the cone to a clean filter paper. If the beach plums are caught in a gelatinous mass, place the contents of the cone in a saucepan, heat until the mass has dissolved, and filter the liquid again.

4. The liquid in the jar is jelly. Cover the jar and let the jelly stand at room temperature for 4 hours, or until it has set. Use the jelly in a recipe or save it for later. Keep in the refrigerator. (If the jelly becomes too tough, stir in boiling water by tablespoons until the desired consistency is obtained. Cook the mixture over lower heat next time. If the jelly remains too thin, place it in a saucepan, boil it for 30 seconds, or until the liquid thickens slightly, pour it into a jar, and let it set again at room temperature.) *Makes about 1⅓ cups.*

Sweetmeats

1. The sticky beach plums left in the filter paper after the jelly has dripped out are sweetmeats. They should be tender and tasty.

2. Use the sweetmeats in a recipe or place them in a covered container. Keep in the refrigerator.

Makes about 2 cups.

Natural Beach Plum Jelly and Candies

2 cups whole beach plums
1½ cups sugar
⅔ cup water

1. Follow the instructions for Natural Beach Plum Jelly made with pitted beach plums, page 33. Note the difference in amounts of sugar and water. This is because a cup of whole beach plums is the equivalent of ¾ cup pitted beach plums.

2. The sticky beach plums left in the filter paper after the jelly has dripped out are candies. Use the candies in a recipe or place them in a covered container. Keep in the refrigerator.

Makes about 1 cup jelly and about 2 cups candies.

Standard Beach Plum Jelly

3½ cups beach plum juice
(see recipe below)
6 cups sugar
½ bottle (3 ounces) liquid pectin
(such as Certo)

1. Place the beach plum juice, sugar, and pectin in a saucepan and mix well. Bring to a boil and boil hard for 1 minute, stirring constantly.
2. Skim off the foam with a spoon or with paper towels. Pour the hot liquid into jars. Cover or seal and let the jelly stand for 4 hours, or until it has set. Use the jelly in a recipe or save it for later. Keep in the refrigerator or, if sterile-packed, on the shelf.
Makes about 4 cups.

BEACH PLUM JUICE

10 cups whole beach plums
2 cups water

1. Place the beach plums in a saucepan, and after they have thawed, crush them with a pestle or a potato masher. Add the water. Simmer, covered, for 30 minutes, or until the beach plums are soft.
2. Filter the juice through a jelly bag suspended over a large measuring cup. (Use a commercial jelly bag or make your own by sewing two layers of muslin or percale around a coat hanger that you have shaped into a circle.) Let the juice drip overnight to obtain the maximum amount. Do not squeeze the fruit. While you get more juice, you also get a cloudy product.
Makes about 3½ cups.

Beach Plum Shrub

Freshly made Beach Plum Shrub has an odor of vinegar, but this will dissipate after a few days. In any case, it does not affect the extraordinarily refreshing taste of the shrub.

> 2 *cups whole beach plums*
> 2 *cups cider vinegar*
> 4 *whole cloves*
> 2 *cups sugar, approximately*

1. Place the beach plums in a jar with a cover, and, after they have thawed, crush them with a pestle or a potato masher. Add the vinegar and cloves. Cover the container and let the combination stand overnight.

2. Pour the liquid into a coffee filter paper (such as Melitta or Chemex), supported in a cone or funnel and placed over a measuring cup. Filter for 1 hour or until the liquid has dripped out. Being careful not to rip the paper, press the beach plums against the sides of the cone to obtain the maximum amount of liquid.

3. Pour the measured liquid into a saucepan. Add an equal amount of sugar. Bring to a boil and boil hard for 1 minute, stirring constantly. Reduce the heat and simmer for 15 minutes, or until the liquid is the consistency of thin syrup.

4. Pour the hot shrub into a bottle. Cover and let cool. Use the shrub in a recipe or save it for later. Keep in the refrigerator.

Makes about 2 cups.

PART FOUR

THE RECIPES

Beach Plums
From Hors d'Oeuvres
To After-Dinner Drinks

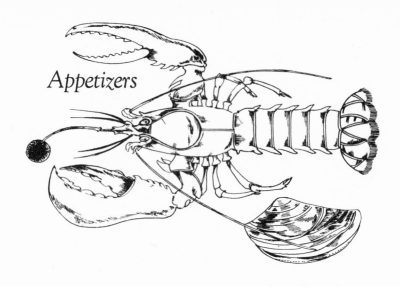

Appetizers

ALPHABET BAKED CLAMS

Anchovies, beach plums, and clams (ABC's) make the tasty stuffing.

1 *2-ounce can flat anchovy fillets*
½ *cup pitted beach plums*
2 *cups shucked raw clams or*
    2 .8-ounce cans minced clams
¼ *cup minced shallots or scallions*
¼ *cup (½ stick) butter*
½ *cup dry breadcrumbs*
2 *teaspoons sugar*
1 *teaspoon thyme*
⅛ *teaspoon pepper*

1. Cut the anchovies and beach plums into small pieces. Mince the raw clams, if using fresh shellfish. Drain the minced clams, if using canned shellfish.

2. Sauté the shallots or scallions in the butter until they are golden. Remove from the heat. Stir in the anchovies, beach plums, clams, breadcrumbs, sugar, thyme, and pepper. Pack the stuffing in buttered clam shells or buttered bakeproof ramekins.

3. If using shells, arrange them on a layer of rock salt or coarse salt in a large baking pan. (The salt supports the shells and conducts the heat.) If using ramekins, place them on a cookie sheet. Bake at 450° for 15 minutes or until the top of the stuffing is light brown and crisp. Serve hot.

Makes 8 servings.

CAPE COCKTAIL

Shellfish with a piquant dipping sauce.

> ½ *cup beach plum jelly*
> ⅔ *cup chili sauce*
> 2 *tablespoons prepared white*
> *horseradish, or to taste*
> 2 *pounds cooked shrimp,*
> *crabmeat, or lobster or*
> *2 dozen raw shucked clams,*
> *oysters, or bay scallops*

1. Mix the beach plum jelly and chili sauce. Add horseradish to taste.

2. Serve as a dipping sauce for the shellfish.

Makes 6 servings.

OLD TOWN HERRING TIDBITS

The herring still run from the creeks to the sea, but the domestic fishing industry does not bother with them. Once local workers bailed thousands of barrels every spring, but now foreign crews net them in the waters off the New England coast. Americans collect only a few for fishmeal. So virtually all our herring is imported—most of it from Canada and Iceland—and in jars. The beach plums in this preparation put the flavor of the shore back into the fish and add delicacy to an otherwise strong hors d'oeuvre.

> 3 *5-ounce jars Bismarck herring fillets*
> 1 *cup whole beach plums*
> 1 *cup sour cream*
> ½ *large purple onion, sliced thin*
> 2 *tablespoons red wine vinegar*
> 1 *tablespoon sugar*
> ½ *teaspoon white pepper*

1. Drain, rinse, and dry the herring fillets. Cut them into pieces. Crush the beach plums with a pestle or potato masher.

2. Place all the ingredients in a jar, cover, and refrigerate. Let stand for two days, stirring occasionally. The beach plums will make the mixture turn pale pink.

Makes 6 servings.

NANTUCKET NUGGETS

An old standby, cocktail meatballs, with a new taste.

½ cup beach plum jelly
½ cup red wine vinegar
1 6-ounce can tomato paste
½ teaspoon chili powder
1 pound lean ground beef
⅓ cup graham cracker crumbs
1 small onion, grated
1 egg, lightly beaten
½ teaspoon ground ginger
½ teaspoon cinnamon
1 teaspoon salt
2 tablespoons vegetable oil

1. Place the beach plum jelly, vinegar, tomato paste, and chili powder in a saucepan. Simmer for 15 minutes, or until the jelly has dissolved and the sauce is slightly thickened. Stir occasionally.

2. Meanwhile, mix the ground meat with the crumbs, onion, egg, ginger, cinnamon, and salt. Shape into small meatballs. Brown in vegetable oil.

3. Add the meatballs to the sauce. Simmer, covered, for 30 minutes, or until the meatballs are firm and fully cooked. Remove the cover and boil for 5 minutes, or until the sauce thickens. Serve hot.

Makes 6 servings.

Soups

VIKING SOUP

Fruit soups, not common American fare, are eaten regularly by Northern Europeans. This recipe is adapted from one given to me by a Norwegian friend. Her grandmother cooked it to warm the family at the winter breakfast table. She set the leftovers by the kitchen door to cool, and then served them with cream for an after-

noon snack or a supper dessert. I often eat Viking Soup
with cottage cheese for lunch.

> 2 tablespoons cornstarch
> 2½ cups water
> 1 tart apple, peeled, cored,
>   and diced
> 4 cups firm dried fruit such as
>   raisins, currants, prunes, or
>   apricots
> 1 teaspoon cinnamon
> ¼ teaspoon ground cloves
> 1½ cups beach plum jelly
> ¼ cup red wine vinegar
> 1 cup walnut pieces

1. In a large saucepan dissolve the cornstarch in ½ cup
of water. Add the remaining 2 cups of water and bring
to a boil. Boil for 2 minutes, stirring constantly, or until
the mixture becomes thick and clear.

2. Add the diced apple, dried fruits, and spices to the
mixture. Simmer for 10 minutes, or until the fruit is
tender, but not soggy. Stir frequently.

3. Add the beach plum jelly and vinegar and simmer
for 5 minutes, or until the jelly has dissolved. Remove
from the heat. Stir in the walnut pieces.

4. Pack in jars and keep in the refrigerator.

Makes about 8 cups.

BARNACLE SOUP

An unusual combination of beach plums and barley, this cold soup makes a good breakfast or late evening snack.

> ¼ *cup barley*
> 3 *cups water*
> 1 *cup beach plum pulp*
> 1 *cup sugar*
> 1 *cinnamon stick*

1. Simmer the barley and water in a covered saucepan for 45 minutes, or until the barley is soft. Drain and rinse.

2. Add the beach plum pulp, sugar, and cinnamon to the soft barley. Cook over moderate heat for 15 minutes or until the soup is thick and clear. Stir frequently to prevent scorching.

3. Remove the cinnamon stick. Serve chilled.

Makes 4 servings.

SOLSTICE SOUP

A midsummer refresher.

> 1 *cup plain yoghurt*
> ⅓ *cup peeled, diced cucumber*
> 2 *tablespoons beach plum jelly*
> 2 *teaspoons red wine vinegar*
>   *diced tomato, green pepper,*
>   *or ham (optional)*

1. Process the yoghurt, cucumber, beach plum jelly, and vinegar in a blender at high speed until liquefied, or force the cucumber through a strainer and combine it with the yoghurt, beach plum jelly, and vinegar.

2. Garnish with tomato, pepper, or ham, if desired. Serve chilled.

Makes 2 servings.

BLOCK ISLAND BROTH

This hot soup is wonderfully warming and very soothing to sore throats.

> 2 *cups beef consommé*
> 2 *tablespoons beach plum shrub*
> *lemon slices*

1. Heat the consommé and beach plum shrub in a saucepan. Do not boil.

2. Pour the broth into mugs. Garnish with lemon slices.

Makes 4 servings.

Fish and Shellfish

ANGLER'S PRIZE

Baked fish plus a spicy stuffing.

> 1 *bluefish or striped bass prepared*
>   *for stuffing (about 4 pounds)*
>   *salt and pepper to taste*
> ¼ *cup pitted beach plums*
> 4 *shallots or scallions (about 2*
>   *tablespoons), minced*
> 2 *cloves garlic, minced*
> 3 *tablespoons butter*
> ⅔ *cup fresh white breadcrumbs*
>   *juice of 2 lemons (about ¼ cup)*
> ¼ *teaspoon red pepper flakes*
> ⅛ *teaspoon ground ginger*

1. Rub the cavity of the fish with salt and pepper. Cut the beach plums into small pieces.

2. Sauté the shallots or scallions and garlic in 2 tablespoons of the butter until they are golden. Remove from the heat. Stir in the beach plums, breadcrumbs, juice of one of the lemons, red pepper, and ginger.

3. Pack the stuffing into the cavity of the fish. Sprinkle the skin with the juice of the second lemon, and dot it with the remaining tablespoon of butter.

4. Bake at 450° for 45 minutes or until the fish flakes easily with a fork but remains moist.

Makes 4 servings.

SALMON MARITIMA

The beach plums add zest to the broth.

> ½ *cup whole beach plums*
> 1 *small onion, halved*
> 1 *small rib of celery with leaves*
> 1 *bay leaf*
> 6 *peppercorns*
> 1 *teaspoon thyme*
> ⅔ *cup dry white wine*
> ⅓ *cup water*
> 4 *salmon steaks (about ⅓*
>   *pound each)*
>   *salt and white pepper to taste*
> 1 *tablespoon butter*
>   *parsley*

1. Place the beach plums, onion, celery, bay leaf, peppercorns, thyme, wine, and water in an enamel or stainless steel saucepan. (The broth, since it contains white wine, will discolor in aluminum.) Simmer for 30 minutes, or until the beach plums are soft.

2. Meanwhile, season the salmon steaks with salt and

pepper, and place them in a buttered enamel or stainless steel frying pan.

3. Strain the broth over the fish, mashing the beach plums against the strainer to obtain the maximum amount of pulp.

4. Simmer, covered, on top of the stove for 15 minutes or until the fish flakes easily with a fork but remains moist.

5. Arrange the salmon steaks on a warm serving platter. Cover with broth. Garnish with parsley.

Makes 4 servings.

OLD MAINE LOBSTER STEW

This unusual stew, based on a seventeenth-century recipe, is a superb way to use leftover lobster. In fact, I like to cook extra lobsters just for the stew.

1 *cup whole beach plums*
1 *cup dry red wine*
¼ *teaspoon nutmeg*
¼ *teaspoon salt*
½ *cup (one stick) butter*
2 *cups cooked lobster meat*

1. Simmer the beach plums, wine, nutmeg, salt, and ¼ cup of the butter for 30 minutes, or until the beach plums are soft. Do not boil.

2. Meanwhile, cut the lobster meat into small chunks. In a frying pan, sauté the chunks in the remaining ¼ cup of butter until they are golden.

3. Strain the broth into the frying pan, mashing the beach plums against the strainer to obtain the maximum amount of pulp. Simmer for 5 minutes or until the lobster chunks are flavored but not tough.

Makes 2 servings.

PORT CITY SHRIMP

A sweet and sour preparation for shrimp and other fried fish.

> 2 *pounds shrimp*
> 1 *egg, lightly beaten*
> 2 *tablespoons flour*
> *salt and pepper to taste*
> ½ *cup peanut oil*
> 2 *tablespoons cornstarch*
> ½ *cup beach plum shrub*
> 2 *tablespoons soy sauce, preferably Japanese*
> 1 *cup water*
> 1 *green pepper and 1 carrot, sliced (optional)*

1. Peel, devein, rinse, and dry the shrimp.

2. Combine the egg, flour, salt, and pepper in a small bowl. Stir the shrimp into the batter.

3. In a large frying pan, heat the oil to just below boiling (375° on an electric skillet). Drop the shrimp, one at a time, into the hot oil. Fry for 5 minutes, or until the shrimp are golden. Turn once. Drain on paper towels, and place on a warm serving platter.

4. In a saucepan, dissolve the cornstarch in the beach plum shrub. Add the soy sauce and water. Bring to a boil and cook, stirring constantly, for 2 minutes, or until the sauce is thick and clear.

5. Pour the sauce over the shrimp. Garnish with pepper and carrot slices, if desired. Serve immediately.

Makes 4 servings.

Poultry

SAILOR'S CHICKEN

Serve hot for dinner or cold for a picnic lunch.

>2 *frying chickens, cut into serving*
>   *pieces*
>   *juice of 4 limes (about ½ cup)*
>2 *teaspoons tarragon*
>   *salt and white pepper to taste*
>2 *tablespoons butter*
>½ *cup beach plum jelly*
>   *grated rind of 1 lime (about*
>   *1 teaspoon)*

1. Arrange the chicken in a single layer, skin side up, in a roasting pan. Pour the lime juice over the chicken. Sprinkle with the tarragon, salt, and pepper.

2. Bake at 325° for 1½ hours, basting frequently with the pan juices.

3. Combine the beach plum jelly and lime rind. Spoon the mixture over the chicken. Increase the oven temperature to 450° and bake an additional 5 minutes, or until the chicken is glazed.

Makes 6 servings.

ZODIAC CHICKEN

This sauce also adds character to game hens or ducklings.

> 2 *frying chickens, cut into serving*
>   *pieces*
>   *black pepper to taste*
> ⅔ *cup beach plum jelly*
> ⅓ *cup beef broth*
> 2 *tablespoons soy sauce, preferably*
>   *Japanese*
> ¼ *cup red wine vinegar*
> 1 *teaspoon dry mustard*
> ⅛ *teaspoon ground cloves*

1. Arrange the chicken in a single layer, skin side up, in a roasting pan. Sprinkle with the pepper.

2. Simmer the beach plum jelly, broth, soy sauce, vinegar, mustard, and cloves for 5 minutes, or until the jelly has dissolved.

3. Paint the chicken with half of the sauce. Bake at 325° for 1½ hours, basting frequently with the remaining half of the sauce.

Makes 6 servings.

ORIENT POINT CHICKEN

A thick beach plum sauce coats the chicken in this Chinese-style dish.

> 1½ *pounds boneless chicken breasts*
> *(about 3 whole breasts)*
> ¼ *cup soy sauce, preferably Japanese*
> ¼ *cup dry sherry*
> 1 *teaspoon ground ginger*
> ⅛ *teaspoon cayenne pepper*
> 2 *tablespoons peanut oil*
> ¼ *cup beach plum pulp*
> 2 *tablespoons peach pulp (strained*
> *babyfood or puréed frozen*
> *peaches)*
> 2 *tablespoons sugar*

1. Remove the skin from the chicken breasts and cut them into small chunks.

2. Combine the soy sauce, sherry, ginger, and cayenne pepper in a small bowl. Stir the chicken into the mixture and marinate for 2 hours at room temperature.

3. Drain and dry the chicken, reserving the marinade. In a frying pan, heat the oil and brown the chicken quickly on all sides.

4. Stir the beach plum pulp, peach pulp, and sugar into the reserved marinade and add the mixture to the frying pan. Simmer, covered, for 3 minutes or until the chicken is tender. Remove the cover and boil for 1 minute or until the sauce thickens. Serve with rice.

Makes 4 servings.

ANCHOR DUCKLING

This dish, a dinner-party mainstay, is based on a recipe given to me years ago by one of my favorite cooks.

> 2 *ducklings, quartered (the butcher can saw*
> *the frozen ducklings for you)*
> *salt and pepper to taste*
> 1½ *cups whole beach plums*
> 1 *cup dark brown sugar*
> *juice of 4 oranges (about 2 cups)*
> *juice of 2 lemons (about ¼ cup)*
> *grated rind of 1 orange (about 1*
> *tablespoon)*
> 2 *tablespoons fruit brandy or*
> *liqueur (such as beach plum,*
> *plum, orange, or cherry)*

1. Thaw, rinse, and dry the duckling quarters. Rub with salt and pepper. Arrange the quarters in a single layer, skin side up, in a large roasting pan or in 2 disposable aluminum roasting pans.

2. Simmer the beach plums, sugar, orange juice, and lemon juice, covered, for 30 minutes or until the beach plums are soft. Strain into a saucepan, mashing the beach plums against the strainer to obtain the maximum amount of pulp. Add the orange rind.

3. Paint the ducklings with ½ cup of the beach plum mixture. Roast at 325° for 4 hours, without basting or pricking, or until the ducklings are very crisp and brown. Because the ducklings are quartered, the excess fat will drip off. The flesh, however, will keep moist.

4. Shortly before serving, boil the remaining beach plum mixture for 15 minutes or until it is clear and slightly thickened. Add the brandy or liqueur, flaming it at the table if desired. Serve the sauce separately.

Makes 8 servings.

HARVEST STUFFING

For a mellow roast chicken, turkey, duck, goose, or game hen.

3 *slices whole wheat bread*
1 *large tart apple, peeled, cored, and diced*
3 *ribs celery, diced*
6 *tablespoons butter*
1 *cup pitted beach plums*
1 *teaspoon cinnamon*
1 *teaspoon ground sage*
¼ *teaspoon ground ginger*
2 *tablespoons light brown sugar*
½ *teaspoon salt*
¼ *cup brandy*

1. Trim the crusts and cut the bread into 1-inch squares. Spread the squares on a cookie sheet and bake them at 200° for 30 minutes, or until they are dry.

2. Meanwhile, sauté the apple and celery in the butter. Add the beach plums, cinnamon, sage, ginger, sugar, and salt, and simmer, covered, for 5 minutes or until the fruits are tender.

3. Remove from the heat. Stir in the brandy and the bread squares.

Makes about 3 cups or enough for a 6-pound bird.

Meats

POTTED BEEF BUCHWALD

Named for the columnist Art Buchwald, who is fond of good food, Martha's Vineyard, and things piquant.

     1 *pot roast, whole or cut into*
         2-inch cubes (about 4 pounds)
     2 *tablespoons olive oil*
     1 *cup whole beach plums*
     2 *medium onions, sliced thin*
    ½ *cup dry red wine*
     1 *cup beef broth*
     1 *bay leaf, crushed*
    ½ *teaspoon allspice*
    ¼ *teaspoon ground ginger*
       salt and pepper to taste
     2 *tablespoons flour*

1. Heat the oil in a large casserole. Brown the meat on all sides. Remove the excess oil with paper towels. Add the beach plums, onions, wine, broth, bay leaf, allspice, ginger, salt, and pepper.

2. Bring to a boil. Then reduce the heat and simmer, covered, on top of the stove for 4 hours if preparing a roast or 2 hours if preparing a stew, or until the meat can be pierced easily with a fork.

3. Place the meat on a warm serving platter. Strain the gravy into a saucepan. Skim off the fat. Mix the flour with ¼ cup of the gravy and return it to the saucepan. Boil for 5 minutes or until thickened. Serve the gravy separately if preparing a roast or pour it over the meat if preparing a stew.

Makes 6 servings.

CANAAN LAMB

The marinade has a Middle Eastern flavor.

> ½ cup whole beach plums
> 2 cloves garlic, minced
> juice of 4 lemons (about ½ cup)
> 2 tablespoons olive oil
> 2 teaspoons ground coriander
> 1 tablespoon salt
> ½ teaspoon ground black pepper
> 1 leg of lamb, butterflied or
> cut into 1½-inch cubes (about
> 4 pounds)

1. Crush the beach plums with a pestle or potato masher. Combine the beach plums, garlic, lemon juice, oil, coriander, salt, and pepper in a shallow baking pan.

2. Place the lamb in the marinade and let it stand for 4 hours at room temperature or overnight in the refrigerator. Turn or stir occasionally.

3. Set the butterflied lamb on a rack or thread the cubes on skewers and place in a roasting pan. Broil, turning once, for 30 minutes if preparing butterflied lamb or 15 minutes if preparing cubes, or until the lamb is crusty and tender. Baste occasionally with the marinade.

Makes 6 servings.

RED RIDING HOOD LAMB

Named for its beautiful red coat.

1 *leg of lamb, tail bone removed*
    (about 6 pounds)
¼ *cup beach plum jelly*
⅓ *cup ketchup*
    juice of 2 lemons (about ¼ cup)
2 *tablespoons olive oil*
½ *teaspoon ground oregano*
    salt and pepper to taste
2 *tablespoons flour*
¾ *cup beef broth*

1. Trim the excess fat from the lamb. Make small gashes in the remaining fat with a paring knife.

2. Simmer the beach plum jelly, ketchup, lemon juice, oil, oregano, salt, and pepper for 3 minutes or until the jelly has dissolved. Reserve ¼ cup of the glaze for the gravy.

3. Paint the lamb with an additional ¼ cup of the glaze, and let it stand for two hours at room temperature.

4. Roast the lamb at 325°, allowing 15 minutes per pound for medium rare. Baste frequently with the remaining glaze. Place the lamb on a warm serving platter and let it stand while making the gravy.

5. Mix the flour into the reserved glaze. Add the broth and boil for 5 minutes, stirring frequently, or until the gravy thickens. Serve the gravy separately.

Makes about 8 servings.

FIRE ISLAND CURRY

The beach plum pulp cuts the hot taste of the curry, so you can be lavish in your use of spices.

> 2 *tablespoons solid white vegetable shortening (such as Crisco)*
> 1 *small onion, diced*
> 1 *clove garlic, minced*
> 1 *teaspoon ground ginger*
> 1 *tablespoon ground cumin*
> 1½ *teaspoons ground coriander*
> ½ *teaspoon cinnamon*
> ¼ *teaspoon chili powder or to taste*
> 2 *pounds beef or lamb cut in 1-inch cubes (leftover rare meat can be used)*
> 2 *teaspoons salt*
> ¼ *cup beach plum pulp*
> ¼ *cup water*

1. Heat the shortening in a large frying pan. Brown the onion and garlic in the shortening.

2. Add the ginger, cumin, coriander, cinnamon, and chili powder to the onion and garlic, and fry for 3 minutes, or until the vegetables have absorbed the spice flavors.

3. Brown the meat in the vegetable-spice mixture. Add the salt, beach plum pulp, and water. Simmer, covered, for 30 minutes if using uncooked meat, and 10 minutes if using leftover meat, or until the meat can be pierced easily with a fork. Serve with rice.

Makes 4 servings.

PLUM ISLAND ROAST PORK

The fruit coating makes the meat succulent and flavorful.

> 1 *pork roast, bones cracked (about 4*
> *pounds) or 1 loin of pork, boned*
> *and rolled (about 2 pounds)*
> ⅓ *cup beach plum stew*
> 1 *clove garlic, minced*
> 1 *tablespoon soy sauce, preferably*
> *Japanese*
> 1 *teaspoon dry mustard*
> ¼ *teaspoon ground ginger*
> ⅛ *teaspoon pepper*

1. Trim the excess fat from the pork. Make small gashes in the remaining fat with a paring knife.

2. Combine the beach plum stew, garlic, soy sauce, mustard, ginger, and pepper. Paint the meat with the mixture, and let it stand at room temperature for two hours.

3. Roast the pork at 325°, allowing 45 minutes per pound, for well done.

Makes 6 servings.

BEACH PLUM BONES

This tangy barbecue sauce also suits chicken.

6 *pounds pork spareribs*
1 *medium onion, minced*
2 *cloves garlic, minced*
2 *tablespoons olive oil*
½ *cup beach plum jelly*
½ *cup ketchup*
½ *cup dry vermouth*
2 *teaspoons dry mustard*
¼ *teaspoon chili powder*
½ *teaspoon ground cumin*
   salt and pepper to taste

1. Cut the spareribs into 8-inch slabs. Place them in a large kettle or casserole and cover with water. Simmer for 45 minutes, or until tender but not fully cooked.

2. Drain and dry. Arrange the slabs in a single layer in a large roasting pan.

3. In a saucepan, sauté the onion and garlic in the oil until golden. Add the beach plum jelly, ketchup, vermouth, mustard, chili powder, cumin, salt, and pepper. Simmer, covered, for 15 minutes, or until the onion is soft.

4. Pour the sauce over the spareribs. Bake at 400° for 30 minutes or until the meat is fully cooked and nicely glazed.

Makes 6 servings.

HAM UNCATENA

This reliable meat sauce, like the ferry that runs between Woods Hole and Martha's Vineyard, is packed full. It can be used on tongue and Canadian bacon slices as well as on ham.

½ cup pitted beach plums
¼ cup raisins
¼ cup dark brown sugar
1 teaspoon dry mustard
¼ teaspoon ground ginger
⅛ teaspoon ground cloves
4 drops red pepper sauce (such as Tabasco)
   juice of ½ orange (about ¼ cup)
⅓ cup dry red wine
⅓ cup fruit brandy or liqueur
      (such as beach plum, plum,
      orange, or cherry)
¼ cup pecan pieces
2 tablespoons peanut oil
6 thick slices boneless, cooked ham
      (about 2 pounds)

1. Place the beach plums, raisins, sugar, mustard, ginger, cloves, red pepper sauce, orange juice, wine, and brandy or liqueur in a saucepan. Simmer, stirring occasionally, for 20 minutes or until the sauce is clear and slightly thickened.

2. Meanwhile, brown the pecan pieces in the oil, taking care not to burn them. Remove the pieces with a slotted spoon, drain them on paper towels, and add them to the sauce.

3. Sauté the ham slices in the oil in which the pecans

were browned, turning once. Arrange the slices on a warm serving platter. Serve the sauce separately.

Makes 6 servings.

VEAL MORSELS

Meats were often cooked with tart fruits in colonial times. This up-to-date dish of veal, lemons, and beach plums is especially satisfying.

>   3 *pounds veal, cut into 2-inch cubes*
>   ¼ *cup flour*
>   *salt and pepper to taste*
>   ¼ *cup (½ stick) butter*
>   1 *medium onion, sliced thin*
>   2 *lemons, peeled, seeded, and diced*
>   2 *cloves garlic, minced*
>   ½ *teaspoon dried rosemary leaves*
>   ⅔ *cup dry white wine*
>   ⅓ *cup beach plum candies or*
>   *beach plum sweetmeats*
>   *grated rind of 1 lemon (about 2*
>   *teaspoons)*

1. Dredge the veal in the flour mixed with the salt and pepper. In a heavy enamel casserole heat the butter, and brown the meat on all sides.

2. Add the onion, lemons, garlic, rosemary, and wine to the casserole. Simmer, covered, for 1¼ hours or until the meat is almost tender. Stir occasionally.

3. Add the beach plum candies or sweetmeats and lemon rind, and simmer an additional 15 minutes or until the fruit is soft and the meat can be pierced easily with a fork.

Makes 6 servings.

VON WANGENHEIM VEAL

This cold dish is named for F. A. J. von Wangenheim, once credited with identifying the species *Prunus maritima*.

1 cup whole beach plums
3 cups white vinegar
3 cups water
4 small onions, halved
2 bay leaves
15 peppercorns
6 whole cloves
1 teaspoon salt
1 boneless rump or leg of veal
   (about 4 pounds)
   prepared mustard, preferably
   Dijon

1. Simmer the beach plums, vinegar, water, onions, bay leaves, peppercorns, cloves, and salt in a casserole for 30 minutes or until the fruit is soft.

2. Remove from the heat and immerse the veal in the hot liquid. (It is not necessary to strain the liquid.) Cover when cool. Marinate in the refrigerator for 4 days, turning daily.

3. Simmer the veal in the marinade for 2½ hours or until tender. Let the veal cool in the liquid. Remove the veal and discard the liquid. Chill the veal and slice thin. Serve with mustard.

Makes 6 servings.

Vegetables

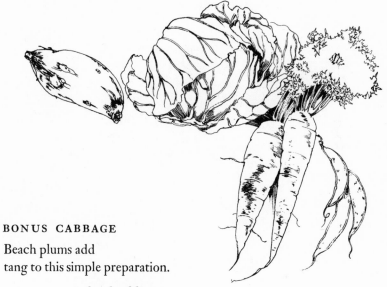

BONUS CABBAGE

Beach plums add
tang to this simple preparation.

1 *head cabbage*
½ *cup beach plum candies or beach*
   plum sweetmeats
2 *tablespoons butter*
  salt and white pepper to taste

1. Shred the cabbage. Rinse and drain, but do not dry it.

2. Place the cabbage, beach plum candies or sweetmeats, butter, salt, and pepper in a saucepan. Simmer, covered, for 15 minutes, or until the cabbage is tender, but not soggy, and the fruit is soft. Stir occasionally.

Makes 6 servings.

MARBLEHEAD CARROTS

An unbeatable vegetable combination.

6 *medium carrots, peeled*
2 *tablespoons butter*
½ *cup beach plum stew*
juice of 1 lemon
(about 2 tablespoons)
⅛ *teaspoon ground cloves*
⅛ *teaspoon ground ginger*
salt and pepper to taste

1. Cut the carrots, crosswise, into slices about ⅜-inch thick. Melt the butter in a large frying pan. Arrange the carrots in a single layer.

2. Spread the beach plum stew over the carrots. Sprinkle with the lemon juice, cloves, ginger, salt, and pepper.

3. Simmer, covered, for 20 minutes, or until the carrot slices are tender, but not soggy. Remove the cover and boil briefly to thicken the sauce.

Makes 6 servings.

MYSTIC PEAS

An intriguing mixture.

2 *10-ounce packages frozen peas or*
2 cups fresh, shelled peas
¼ *cup (½ stick) butter*
¼ *cup beach plum jelly*
¼ *cup chopped chives*
salt and pepper to taste

1. Thaw the peas, if using frozen produce. Parboil the peas for 3 minutes, if using fresh produce. Drain and dry the peas.

2. Melt the butter in a large frying pan. Simmer the peas, uncovered, for 3 minutes.

3. Add the beach plum jelly, chives, salt, and pepper. Simmer an additional 3 minutes, or until the jelly has dissolved and the chives are soft.

Makes 6 servings.

SWEET POTATO PARFAIT

Luscious layers of sweet potatoes, pineapple, and beach plums.

> 2 *pounds fresh sweet potatoes or*
> *yams or 2 16-ounce cans sweet*
> *potatoes or yams*
> 1 *teaspoon cinnamon*
> 2 *cups diced fresh pineapple or 1*
> *20-ounce can unsweetened*
> *crushed pineapple*
> ½ *teaspoon mace*
> 2 *tablespoons butter*
> 1 *cup beach plum stew*

1. If using fresh produce, boil the sweet potatoes or yams in their jackets for 45 minutes, or until they can be pierced easily with a fork. Cool and peel them. If using canned produce, drain the sweet potatoes or yams.

2. Mash the sweet potatoes or yams only until they are

lumpy, not completely smooth, in consistency. Combine with the cinnamon.

3. Drain the fresh or canned pineapple. Combine with the mace.

4. Butter a 2-quart casserole. Spread the sweet potatoes or yams in a layer, cover with the pineapple, and top with the peach plum stew. Bake at 350° for 1 hour, or until the sweet potatoes or yams and pineapple are very hot and the beach plum stew is syrupy.

Makes 8 servings.

SPICED SQUASH

This vegetable is a treat to the eye as well as to the palate.

> 2 *small acorn or butternut*
>   *squashes*
> 1 *cup pitted beach plums*
> 1 *tablespoon butter*
>   *juice of 1 lemon*
>   *(about 2 tablespoons)*
> 1⅓ *cups sugar*
> 1½ *teaspoons cinnamon*
> ¼ *teaspoon nutmeg*
> ¼ *teaspoon allspice*
>   *salt to taste*

1. Quarter the squashes, and parboil the quarters for 10 minutes. Peel and cut into 1-inch cubes.

2. Place the squash cubes and beach plums in a buttered, 9-inch pie dish. Sprinkle with the lemon juice. Combine the sugar, cinnamon, nutmeg, and allspice, and pour the mixture over the squash cubes and beach plums.

3. Bake at 300° for 1 hour, or until the squash is glazed and tender. Baste occasionally with the pan juices.

Makes 8 servings.

Sauces

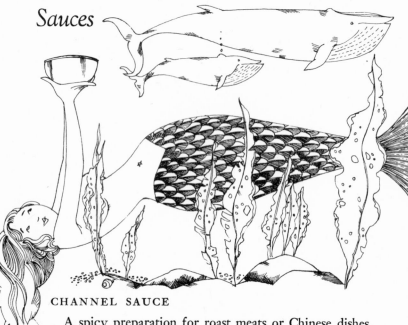

CHANNEL SAUCE

A spicy preparation for roast meats or Chinese dishes.

> 2 *tablespoons beach plum pulp,*
>   *strained*
> 2 *tablespoons dry mustard*
> 2 *tablespoons soy sauce, preferably*
>   *Japanese*
> 2 *tablespoons confectioners' sugar*

1. In a small bowl, mix the ingredients with a fork until they are thoroughly blended. The sauce should be the consistency of thin mustard.

2. Let the sauce stand for 5 minutes to allow the flavors to blend.

Makes about ⅓ cup or 4 servings.

BAY SAUCE

A heady combination.

> 1 *cup beach plum jelly*
> ½ *cup rum*

1. Place the ingredients in a saucepan. Heat, without boiling, for 5 minutes, or until the beach plum jelly has dissolved. Let cool.
2. Serve with ice cream or fruit. Bay sauce keeps indefinitely in the refrigerator.

Makes about 1½ cups or 12 servings.

DELAWARE SAUCE

A rich dressing.

> 1 *cup sour cream*
> ½ *cup beach plum jelly*
> 1 *tablespoon lemon juice*

1. In a small bowl, beat the ingredients with a fork until they are thoroughly blended.
2. Serve with fruit.

Makes about 1½ cups or 12 servings.

MERMAID SAUCE

Elusive flavoring.

> ½ *cup beach plum jelly*
> ½ *cup fruit brandy or liqueur*
>   *(such as beach plum, plum,*
>   *orange, or cherry)*
> ¼ *cup honey*
> ¼ *cup lemon juice*

1. Place the ingredients in a saucepan. Heat, without boiling, for 3 minutes, or until the beach plum jelly has dissolved. Let cool.

2. Serve with fruit. Mermaid Sauce keeps indefinitely in the refrigerator.

Makes about 1½ cups or 12 servings.

BEACH PLUM SYRUP

A refreshing accompaniment to pancakes, crêpes, or French toast.

> 1 *cup beach plum jelly*
> ⅓ *cup water*
> ⅓ *cup sugar*
> 3 *2-inch strips orange peel*

1. In a saucepan, simmer the ingredients for 30 minutes, or until the beach plum jelly and sugar have dissolved and the orange flavor has infused. Skim off the foam with a spoon, or with paper towels.

2. Remove the orange peel and pour the syrup into a bottle. Keep in the refrigerator.

Makes about 1½ cups or 12 servings.

BARBECUE SAUCE:
See Beach Plum Bones, page 65.

COCKTAIL SAUCE:
See Cape Cocktail, page 41.

SWEET AND SOUR SAUCE:
See Port City Shrimp, page 51.

Preserves

BEACH PLUM BUTTER

Good with roast meats, as a stuffing for baked apples, or, of course, on toast.

> 2 *cups beach plum pulp*
> 1 *cup granulated sugar*
> 1 *cup light brown sugar*
> 1 *teaspoon cinnamon*
> ½ *teaspoon nutmeg*
> ½ *teaspoon allspice*

1. Place the ingredients in a saucepan. Cook slowly, stirring frequently, for 30 minutes or until the mixture becomes thick and clear.

2. Pour the butter into jars. Cover or seal and let cool. Keep in the refrigerator or, if sterile-packed, on the shelf. *Makes about 2 cups.*

BEACH PLUM JAM

Beach Plum Stew and Beach Plum Butter are, occasionally, misnamed "Jam." The "Jam" label should be pasted only on a jar of preserves made with minced or mashed fruit.

   2 *cups pitted beach plums*
   2 *cups sugar*
  ⅓ *cup water*
  ⅓ *cup orange juice*

1. Cut the beach plums into small pieces. Place the ingredients in a saucepan. Bring the mixture to a boil. Reduce the heat and simmer for 30 minutes, or until the fruit is soft and the liquid is the consistency of thin syrup. Stir occasionally.

2. Pour the jam into jars. Cover or seal and let cool. Keep in the refrigerator, or, if sterile-packed, on the shelf.

Makes about 2 cups.

GRAND PORTAGE CHUTNEY

This relish complements roast meats and curries.

   1 *cup pitted beach plums*
   1 *lemon*
   4 *cloves garlic, minced*
  ½ *cup raisins*
   1 *cup sugar*
   1 *cup white vinegar*
   2 *tablespoons water*
   1 *teaspoon ground ginger*
   2 *teaspoons salt*

1. Cut the beach plums into pieces. Peel, seed, and dice the lemon.

2. Place the beach plums, the lemon, and the remaining ingredients in a saucepan. Cook slowly, stirring frequently, for 30 minutes, or until the beach plums are soft.

3. Pour the chutney into jars. Cover or seal and let cool. Keep in the refrigerator, or, if sterile-packed, on the shelf. Let the chutney stand for 2 weeks before using it to allow the flavors to blend.

Makes about 2 cups.

BEACH PLUM JELLY:
See page 31.

BEACH PLUM STEW:
See page 30.

MEAT RELISH:
See Viking Soup, page 44.

MOZART OMELETTE

Variation on a standard theme.

> ¼ cup beach plum stew
> 2 sausages, cooked and chopped
>   (about 2 ounces meat)
> ¼ cup candied citron, diced
> ¼ cup pine nuts or chopped,
>   blanched almonds
> ¼ teaspoon cinnamon
> 6 eggs
>   salt and white pepper to taste
> 4 tablespoons (½ stick) butter

1. Mix the beach plum stew, sausages, citron, nuts, and cinnamon in a small bowl.

2. Beat the eggs lightly with a fork. Season with the salt and pepper. Heat 1 tablespoon of the butter in an omelette pan or small frying pan. When the butter is very hot, but not browned, pour in ¼ of the eggs (the equivalent of 1½ eggs). Tilt the pan so that the eggs are evenly distributed.

3. When the eggs are firm, but still slightly moist on top, spoon ¼ of the beach plum filling (about ⅓ cup) across the center of the omelette. Fold in thirds with a spatula. The procedure should take about 1½ minutes.

4. Place the omelette on a warm serving platter, and repeat the procedure 3 more times until all the eggs and filling are used. Serve immediately.

Makes 4 servings.

SCHUBERT OMELETTE

The beach plum jelly, orange rind, and cottage cheese are a lyrical trio.

> ¼ *cup beach plum jelly*
> 1 *teaspoon grated orange rind*
> ⅓ *cup small curd, creamed*
>   *cottage cheese*
> 6 *eggs*
>   *salt to taste*
> 4 *tablespoons (½ stick) butter*

1. Combine the beach plum jelly, orange rind, and cottage cheese to make the filling.

2. Beat the eggs lightly with a fork. Season with the salt. Heat 1 tablespoon of the butter in an omelette pan or small frying pan. When the butter is very hot, but not browned, pour in ¼ of the eggs (the equivalent of 1½ eggs). Tilt the pan so that the eggs are evenly distributed.

3. When the eggs are firm, but still slightly moist on top, spoon ¼ of the filling (about 2 tablespoons) across the center of the omelette. Fold in thirds with a spatula. The procedure should take about 1½ minutes.

4. Place the omelette on a warm serving platter, and repeat the procedure 3 more times until all the eggs and filling are used. Serve immediately.

Makes 4 servings.

GOOD MORNING MUFFINS

When was the last time you had homemade muffins for breakfast? If you prepare the dry ingredients at night, you can finish without a fuss in the morning. The muffins will be ready with the coffee, and they will keep you going long after the caffeine has worn off.

  1 *cup sifted all-purpose flour*
  1 *cup whole wheat flour*
  ½ *cup wheat germ*
  ¼ *cup sugar*
  1 *tablespoon baking powder*
  1 *teaspoon salt*
  2 *eggs*
  1 *cup milk*
  ¼ *cup (½ stick) butter, melted*
  1½ *cups beach plum sweetmeats*

1. Combine the flours, wheat germ, sugar, baking powder, and salt.

2. Beat the eggs lightly with a fork. Add the milk and melted butter. Stir the liquid into the dry ingredients until they are just blended. The batter will be heavy and slightly lumpy. Fold in the beach plum sweetmeats.

3. Spoon the batter into greased muffin cups, or ungreased, nonstick muffin cups. The cups should be about ⅔ full. Bake in a preheated 400° oven for 15 minutes, or until the tops of the muffins are golden.

Makes 12 muffins.

SPINNAKERS

Sweet muffins for afternoon or evening tea.

> ¼ cup (½ stick) butter
> ½ cup sugar
> 1 egg
> ¼ cup milk
> 1 cup sifted flour
> 1 teaspoon baking powder
> ¼ teaspoon salt
> 1 cup beach plum sweetmeats

1. Have all the ingredients at room temperature. Cream the butter and sugar. Add the egg and milk and beat well.
2. Combine the flour, baking powder, and salt. Add to the liquid mixture, stirring until the ingredients are just blended. Fold in the beach plum sweetmeats.
3. Spoon the batter into greased muffin cups, or ungreased nonstick muffin cups. The cups should be about ⅔ full. Bake in a preheated 375° oven for 15 minutes or until the tops of the muffins are golden.

Makes 6 muffins.

POST HOUSE COFFEE CAKES

The beach plum fillings are new, but the doughs are old family favorites.

CRUMBLY BEACH PLUM FILLING

⅔ *cup beach plum sweetmeats,*
    cut into pieces
⅔ *cup chopped walnuts or pecans*
⅔ *cup sugar*
1 *teaspoon cinnamon*

CRUNCHY BEACH PLUM FILLING

1 *cup beach plum sweetmeats,*
    cut into pieces
½ *cup candied citron, chopped*
½ *cup sugar*
1 *teaspoon ground cardamom*

1. Mix the ingredients in a small bowl.
2. Use in chosen coffee cake recipe.
Makes about 1½ cups, or enough to fill the following coffee cakes.

GRANDMOTHER'S SOUR CREAM DOUGH

2½ *cups sifted flour*
½ *cup sugar*
1½ *teaspoons baking powder*
1 *teaspoon baking soda*
⅛ *teaspoon salt*
½ *cup (1 stick) butter*
1 *egg*
½ *cup sour cream*
¼ *cup (½ stick) butter, melted*
    (optional)

1. Combine the flour, sugar, baking powder, baking soda, and salt. Cut in the butter with a fork or with a pastry blender until the mixture resembles fine crumbs. Beat in the eggs and sour cream.

2. Working with floured hands, shape the dough into 2 balls. Roll on a floured pastry cloth into the shape of a rectangle ¼ inch thick. Spread with chosen filling. Roll up the dough.

3. Place on a lightly greased cookie sheet with the seam on the underside. Paint with melted butter if browned, glazed coffee cakes are desired.

4. Bake in a preheated 325° oven for 30 minutes, or until the dough is firm but remains moist. Let cool and cut into slices.

Makes about 16 slices.

GREAT GRANDMOTHER'S PASTRY DOUGH

> 1 *cup (2 sticks) butter*
> 3 *egg yolks*
> 1 *cup (½ pint) light cream or milk*
> 1 *envelope or 1 cake yeast*
> 3 *cups sifted flour*
> 1 *egg white, lightly beaten*
>   *(optional)*

1. Warm the cream or milk, and dissolve the yeast in it. (The cream or milk should be body temperature. Test it by dabbing a few drops on your wrist.) Add the cream or milk to the butter and egg yolk mixture and beat well.

2. Stir in the flour, mixing until the dough begins to pull

away from the sides of the bowl. Cover the dough with a dishtowel and let it rest in the refrigerator for 6 hours or overnight.

3. Shape the dough into 3 balls, working in more flour if necessary for rolling. Roll on a floured pastry cloth into the shape of a circle about ¼ inch thick. Cut the circle into 12 pie-shaped wedges, but do not separate the wedges. Spread the entire circle with chosen filling. Starting from the circumference, roll each wedge to the center.

4. Shape each rolled wedge into a crescent and place it on a lightly greased cookie sheet with the point tucked under. Paint with egg white if browned, glazed coffee cakes are desired.

5. Bake in a preheated 400° oven for 20 minutes, or until the dough is firm.

Makes about 36 crescents.

Baked Desserts

SUGAR PLUM DROPS

Melt-in-your-mouth treats.

> ½ cup (1 stick) butter
> ½ cup sugar
> 1 egg
> ½ teaspoon vanilla extract
> ½ cup beach plum stew
> 1⅔ cups sifted flour
> 1 teaspoon baking powder
> ½ cup confectioners' sugar

1. Cream the butter and sugar. Add the egg and vanilla extract. Beat in the beach plum stew.

2. Combine the flour and baking powder. Stir the dry ingredients into the beach plum mixture.

3. Drop the dough by teaspoons onto a greased cookie sheet or ungreased nonstick cookie sheet. Bake in a pre-heated 375° oven for 10 minutes, or until the cookies are golden at the edges.

4. Cool on a rack. (An old refrigerator shelf placed across the sink makes a good cooling rack. Remember not to run the water.) Dust with confectioners' sugar. Store in a tightly covered container.

Makes about 4 dozen cookies.

PROSELYTE CAKE

Cake eaters love it, and cookie eaters are converted.

> ¾ *cup (1 stick) butter, preferably*
>   *unsalted*
> 1½ *cups sugar*
> 3 *eggs*
> 1½ *teaspoons almond extract*
> 2 *cups beach plum stew*
> 3 *cups sifted flour*
> ⅔ *cup simple frosting, approximately*
>   *(see recipe below)*

1. Have all the ingredients at room temperature. Cream the butter and sugar. Add the eggs and beat until the mixture is pale and fluffy. Beat in the almond extract and 1½ cups of the beach plum stew.

2. Stir the flour into the beach plum mixture.

3. Line the bottoms of two 8-inch cake pans with lightly buttered waxed paper. Pour the batter into them, spreading it evenly with a scraper. Bake in a preheated 325° oven for 1¼ hours, or until the layers are browned and very firm to the touch. Let cool. Remove the layers from the pans. Peel off the waxed paper.

4. Spread the remaining ½ cup of beach plum stew between the layers. Cover the top with Simple Frosting.
Makes 10 servings.

SIMPLE FROSTING

> 2 *cups confectioners' sugar*
> 2 *tablespoons butter, preferably*
>   *unsalted*
> 3 *tablespoons water, approximately*

1. Beat the confectioners' sugar, butter, and 2 tablespoons of the water with a fork or in an electric mixer until the frosting is stiff and smooth.
2. Beat in the remaining water by teaspoons, stopping when the frosting is the right consistency for spreading.
Makes about ⅔ cup.

SAND BARS

They are gone with the change of the tide.

> 1 *cup (2 sticks) butter*
> 1 *cup dark brown sugar*
> 2 *cups sifted flour*
> ½ *teaspoon baking soda*
> ½ *teaspoon salt*
> 1½ *cups quick or instant oats*
> 1 *cup beach plum stew*

1. Cream the butter and sugar. Combine the flour, baking soda, and salt. Stir the dry ingredients into the creamed mixture. Stir in the oats.

2. Press ⅔ of the dough into the bottom of a 9- x 13-inch baking pan. Heat the beach plum stew until it is soft and spread it over the dough. Crumble the remaining ⅓ of the dough over the beach plum stew.

3. Bake in a preheated 425° oven for 30 minutes or until firm and lightly browned. Cut into bars while the dough is still warm, but not oven hot. Cool in the pan. Store in a tightly covered container.

Makes about 30 bars.

HUMPHRY MARSHALL PIE

Dedicated to the man who named the beach plum.

> 4 *eggs*
> ½ *cup (1 stick) butter, melted*
> 1½ *cups light brown sugar*
> 1 *cup beach plum stew*
> 1 *pie crust, unbaked (see*
> *recipe below)*

1. Beat the eggs. Add the melted butter. Mix in the sugar and the beach plum stew.

2. Pour the filling into an unbaked pie crust, making sure

the pieces of fruit are distributed throughout the pie. Bake in a preheated 350° oven for 45 minutes, or until the crust is golden and the filling is brown and firm.

Makes 8 servings.

FAVORITE PIE CRUST

> 1¼ *cups flour*
> ¼ *teaspoon baking powder*
> ¼ *teaspoon salt*
> ½ *cup solid white vegetable*
>   *shortening (such as Crisco)*
> 2 *tablespoons ice water,*
>   *approximately*

1. Combine the flour, baking powder, and salt. With a fork, cut in ¼ cup of the shortening, working until the mixture is the consistency of fine crumbs. Cut in the remaining ¼ cup of the shortening, stopping when the mixture is the consistency of coarse crumbs. Add the

water by teaspoons, mixing with a fork all the time, until the dough just holds together but is not wet or sticky.

2. Refrigerate the dough for ½ hour. Roll on a floured pastry cloth to the thickness of ⅛ inch. Place in a 9-inch pie dish. Trim the crust, fold the edge double and press it with the tines of a fork.

Makes one 9-inch crust.

COASTLINE KUCHEN

This delightful, simple recipe comes from the Pacific coast where it is made with local plums. Atlantic coast cooks can use beach plums. I have adapted the recipe to them.

> 1¼ *cups plus 2 tablespoons flour*
> 2 *tablespoons plus 1 cup sugar*
> ½ *cup (1 stick) butter, melted*
> 1 *tablespoon white vinegar*
> 1½ *cups pitted beach plums*
> 1 *teaspoon cinnamon*
> 2 *eggs, lightly beaten*

1. Combine 1¼ cups of the flour with 2 tablespoons of the sugar. Stir in the melted butter and vinegar. Pat the dough into a 9-inch pie dish, covering the sides as well as the bottom. Prick the bottom of the dough with a fork.

2. Bake in a preheated 400° oven for 10 minutes, or until the dough turns cream-colored and is partially cooked. Sprinkle the partially cooked dough with the remaining 2 tablespoons of flour.

3. Arrange the beach plums on the dough. Combine the remaining 1 cup of sugar and cinnamon and sprinkle over the fruit. Pour the eggs over the sugared fruit, making sure the top area is entirely covered.

4. Bake again at 400° for 40 minutes, or until the crust is golden and the glaze is brown and crisp.

Makes 8 servings.

BLUSHING BETSYS

Too many beach plums, like too much chocolate, can be overpowering. For cobbler-like desserts I prefer a combination of beach plums and apples or peaches. You can use these bases with either of the toppings given, or supply your own favorite. A dollop of ice cream or whipped cream completes the dish.

BEACH PLUM–APPLE BASE

> 2 *cups beach plum sweetmeats*
> 2 *cups diced apples, peeled if*
>   *desired (about 3 large apples)*
> 1 *cup light brown sugar*
>   *grated rind of 1 orange*
>   *(about 1 tablespoon)*

BEACH PLUM–PEACH BASE

> 2 *cups beach plum sweetmeats*
> 2 *cups diced peaches,*
>   *peeled if desired*
>   *(about 6 medium peaches)*
> 1 *cup sugar*
> ½ *teaspoon mace*

1. Mix the ingredients for the chosen base in a small bowl.

2. Place the mixture in a buttered casserole or loaf pan.

Makes about 4 cups or enough for 1 Blushing Betsy.

PUFFY TOPPING

> 1 *cup flour*
> 1 *cup sugar*
> 1 *teaspoon baking powder*
> ½ *teaspoon salt*
> 1 *egg, lightly beaten*
> ¼ *cup (½ stick) butter, melted*
> ½ *teaspoon cinnamon*

1. Combine the flour, sugar, baking powder, and salt. Mix the egg into the dry ingredients. The dough will be heavy and sticky. Spread the dough over the fruit base.

2. Drizzle the melted butter over the dough. Dust with the cinnamon.

3. Bake in a preheated 350° oven for 45 minutes, or until the fruit is tender and the topping is brown.

Makes 6 servings.

CRISPY TOPPING

> ⅓ cup flour
> ¼ cup sugar
> ⅓ cup wheat germ or ground nuts
> ¼ cup (½ stick) butter

1. Combine the flour, sugar, and wheat germ or ground nuts. Blend the butter into the dry ingredients with a fork or with the fingers. Crumble the mixture over the fruit base.

2. Bake in a preheated 350° oven for 45 minutes, or until the fruit is tender and the topping is crisp.

Makes 6 servings.

PILGRIM PUDDING

A pudding made with real plums is exceptional. The traditional Christmas fare is usually laced with raisins, rinds, and spices. It is called a plum pudding because a "sugar plum" or "plum" once meant any kind of dried or candied fruit or peel. In this pudding, beach plums are the only "plums." They combine the sweet taste of dried fruit and the tart flavor of candied peel to make a unique holiday dessert.

1 *cup sifted flour*
1½ *teaspoons baking powder*
⅛ *teaspoon salt*
½ *cup (1 stick) butter*
½ *cup dry breadcrumbs*
1½ *cups sugar*
1 *egg, lightly beaten*
⅔ *cup milk*
1½ *cups beach plum sweetmeats*
1 *cup (½ pint) heavy cream, whipped*
2 *tablespoons fruit brandy or liqueur (such as beach plum, plum, orange, or cherry)*

1. Combine the flour, baking powder, and salt. Cut in the butter, working until the mixture is the consistency of coarse crumbs. Add the breadcrumbs and sugar.

2. Mix the egg and milk together and stir the liquid mixture into the dry ingredients. Fold in the beach plum sweetmeats. Pour the batter into a buttered 2-quart container such as a gelatin mold or charlotte or soufflé dish. The container should be about ⅔ full. Cover tightly with aluminum foil.

3. Fill a kettle large enough to hold the pudding container with 2 inches of water. Place the container in the

water, cover the kettle, and bring the water to a boil. Reduce the heat to simmer, and steam the pudding for 2 hours, or until a knife inserted in the center comes out clean. Add hot water to the kettle occasionally, if necessary.

4. Remove the container from the kettle and let the pudding cool. Unmold if desired. Serve at room temperature with whipped cream flavored with fruit brandy or liqueur.

Makes 8 servings.

Cold Desserts

FRUIT FOAM

An unusual, light dessert.

> 2 *large apples or pears, peeled,*
>   *cored, and diced*
> ½ *cup beach plum jelly*
> 2 *teaspoons powdered whiskey sour mix*
> 2 *tablespoons water, approximately*

1. Process all the ingredients in a blender at high speed until liquefied, adding water if necessary for blending. The mixture will be pink and frothy. (The citric acid in the whiskey sour mix keeps the fruit from turning brown, and the other ingredients provide the flavoring.)
2. Chill. Serve alone or with plain cake.

Makes 4 servings.

SUNSET APPLESAUCE

Beach plums give the applesauce a rosy hue and a fresh, outdoor taste.

> 6 *tart apples, cored and sliced*
> 1 *cup pitted beach plums*
> 1 *cup sugar*
> ½ *cup water*

1. Simmer the ingredients in a large saucepan for 30 minutes or until the fruit is soft, stirring occasionally. Force through a food mill or coarse strainer.

2. Chill. Serve alone or with plain cake.

Makes about 4 cups or 12 servings.

PLUM DELICIOUS SHERBET

A perfect ending for any heavy dinner.

> 2 *cups beach plum pulp*
> 2 *cups sugar*
> 1 *envelope (1 tablespoon) plain*
>   *gelatin*
> *juice of ½ orange (about ¼ cup)*
> 1 *tablespoon grated orange rind*
> 1 *cup (½ pint) heavy cream or*
>   2 *egg whites*

1. Place the beach plum pulp and sugar in a saucepan. Bring to a boil. Reduce the heat and simmer for 10 minutes or until the mixture is dark and clear. Stir constantly.

2. Soften the gelatin in the orange juice. Add to the hot beach plum mixture, stirring until the granules have completely dissolved.

3. Place the mixture in a shallow bowl or tray and freeze for 2 hours, or until mushy. Beat the mushy mixture, preferably with an electric mixer, until it becomes pale and fluffy.

4. If using cream, whip it in a chilled bowl with chilled beaters until it holds soft peaks. If using egg whites, beat them until they hold stiff peaks. Fold the whipped cream or the beaten egg whites into the beach plum mixture.

5. Place the sherbet in a serving bowl and freeze it for 4 hours, or until it is firm.

Makes about 4 cups or 8 servings.

SYLLABUB

A syllabub was a frothy colonial concoction that took several days to prepare. It involved curdling fresh cream with wine and adding sugar and flavoring. This, being a modern adaptation, takes only minutes to make. It is delicious.

> ¼ *cup beach plum jelly*
> ¼ *cup rum*
> 1 *cup (½ pint) heavy cream*
> ¼ *cup confectioners' sugar*

1. Place the beach plum jelly and rum in a saucepan.

Heat, without boiling, for 3 minutes, or until the jelly has dissolved. Let cool.

2. Meanwhile, whip the cream in a chilled bowl with chilled beaters until it begins to thicken. Add the confectioners' sugar gradually, whipping until the cream is stiff but not overbeaten and lumpy.

3. Fold in the beach plum jelly and rum mixture. Spoon into glasses. Refrigerate for no more than 30 minutes, or serve immediately.

Makes 4 servings.

ABSOLUTELY NUTS!

But a tasty combination.

> 1 *pound assorted soft and semi-soft cheeses, such as Camembert or Brie and Gourmandise or Bel Paese*
> 48 *beach plum candies or beach plum sweetmeats*
> 48 *shelled pistachio nuts plain crackers*

1. Arrange the cheeses on a platter and allow them to come to room temperature.

2. If beach plum candies are used, arrange them with the nuts on the cheese platter. If beach plum sweetmeats are used, stuff them with the nuts. Place them on the cheese platter. Serve with crackers.

Makes 6 servings.

FRUIT SALAD

Citrus fruits and other acid fruits, such as peaches, strawberries, and pineapples, are particularly good with beach plum sauces. See pages 74–76 for the recipes.

Beverages

GLOUCESTER GROG

Warm congratulations for winning your battle with the elements.

> 1 *gallon apple cider*
> 1 *cup whole beach plums*
> 6 *whole cloves*
> 12 *cardamom seeds*
> 1 *cinnamon stick*
> ⅘ *quart (1 bottle) bourbon*

1. Simmer the cider, beach plums, cloves, cardamom seeds, and cinnamon stick in a large saucepan or kettle for 1 hour, or until the fruit and spice flavors have infused. The beach plums, cloves, and cardamom seeds may be tied in an all-purpose cloth (such as Handi-Wipes) or in cheesecloth to facilitate their removal.

2. Remove the beach plums and spices. Add the bourbon. Serve hot.

Makes 40 servings.

LIGHTHOUSE TEA

To cut the bitter taste of tea, place a beach plum in the pot with the tea leaves or tea bags. Pour the boiling water into the pot and let the tea steep for 5 minutes. The strong taste is gone, but there is no loss of tea flavor. Why? The reason seems to be that the boiling water releases the pectin from the beach plum and this counteracts the acid of the tea. You can test the method by brewing an ordinary pot of tea, placing a beach plum in one cup, but not in another, and sampling the tea from both cups. The smooth taste of the Lighthouse Tea is unmistakable.

VINEYARD TEA

To restore your spirits after a hard day of beach plum harvesting.

> ½ *cup tea*
> 1 *teaspoon beach plum jelly*
> 2 *tablespoons blended whiskey*

1. Place the ingredients in a saucepan. Heat, without boiling, for 1 minute, or until the beach plum jelly has dissolved.

2. Serve in a mug.

Makes 1 serving.

BEACH PLUM BAVAROISE

The French version of spiked tea is called a bavaroise. In the nineteenth century the bavaroise was a favorite drink of the Salon set. It was cited as a good remedy for chest congestion. To make a beach plum bavaroise, beat a tablespoon of milk and a raw egg yolk into the Vineyard Tea. The drink will be surprisingly light and smooth.

DUNE BUGGY

An exceptional summer drink.

> ¼ *cup dry vermouth*
> 1 *tablespoon beach plum shrub*
> ½ *cup club soda*
> 1 *strip orange peel (optional)*

1. Mix the dry vermouth, beach plum shrub, and club soda. Serve over ice.

2. Garnish with orange peel, if desired.

Makes 1 serving.

PLUMLET

A superior cocktail.

> 3 *tablespoons gin or vodka*
> 1 *tablespoon beach plum shrub*
> 1 *beach plum candy (optional)*

1. Mix the gin or vodka and the beach plum shrub. Serve over ice.

2. Garnish with a beach plum candy, if desired.

Makes 1 serving.

BEACH PLUM SWITCHEL

An old-fashioned, nonalcoholic thirst-quencher.

> ¾ *cup buttermilk*
> 2 *tablespoons beach plum shrub*
> 2 *drops bitters*
> 1 *mint leaf (optional)*

1. Mix the buttermilk, beach plum shrub, and bitters. Chill. Serve in a mug.

2. Garnish with a mint leaf, if desired.

Makes 1 serving.

VELOURS, A BEACH PLUM LIQUEUR

This liqueur, as luxurious as its name suggests, is simple to make and soothing to swallow.

4 *cups whole beach plums*
4 *cups sugar*
⅘ *quart (1 bottle) grain alcohol*
1 *cinnamon stick*
6 *cloves*

1. Clean a large jar with a tight-fitting cover. (Mine happened to be occupied by a toad. I convinced the children to set him free, scrubbed his home with chlorine bleach, rinsed carefully, and counted on the alcohol to do the rest.) Place the beach plums in the jar, add the sugar, and let the combination stand overnight.

2. Add the alcohol and the spices. Cover the jar tightly. Let the mixture stand for at least 2 weeks at room temperature. Open the jar and stir the contents daily with a long-handled spoon or scraper.

3. Strain the liqueur through all-purpose cloth (such as Handi-Wipes) or through cheesecloth, wringing the fruit in the cloth to obtain the maximum amount of liqueur.

4. Filter the liqueur, about 2 cups at a time, through a coffee filter paper (such as Melitta or Chemex), supported in a cone or funnel and placed over a clean jar. If the original paper becomes clogged, and the liquid no longer drips out steadily, transfer the contents of the cone to a clean filter paper. The filtering process may take as long

as 8 hours. If the liqueur is not perfectly clear, filter it again.

5. Store in a tightly covered bottle.

Makes about 1 quart.

PLUM CRAZY BRANDY

This cordial could become your family specialty.

> 2 *cups whole beach plums*
> 2 *cups sugar*
> ⅘ *quart (1 bottle) brandy*

1. Clean a large jar with a tight-fitting cover. Place the beach plums in the jar, add the sugar, and let the combination stand overnight.

2. Add the brandy. (The beach plums will mellow the rough taste of an inexpensive brandy, but you can use fine cognac for a superb result.) Cover the jar tightly. Let the mixture stand for at least 2 weeks at room temperature. Open the jar and stir the contents daily with a long-handled spoon or scraper.

3. Strain the brandy through all-purpose cloth (such as

Handi-Wipes) or through cheesecloth, wringing the fruit in the cloth to obtain the maximum amount of brandy.

4. Filter the brandy, about 2 cups at a time, through a coffee filter paper (such as Melitta or Chemex) supported in a cone or funnel and placed over a clean jar. If the original paper becomes clogged, and the liquid no longer drips out steadily, transfer the contents of the cone to a clean filter paper. The filtering process may take as long as 8 hours. If the brandy is not perfectly clear, filter it again.

5. Store in a tightly covered bottle.

Makes about 1 quart.

WINDJAMMER WINE

This is the way to make a small quantity of beach plum wine according to very simple procedures. To make larger quantities of wine with more attention to the fine points of the art—such as developing water locks, killing off wild yeasts, prolonging the fermenting process, and the like—consult a detailed source. Since home brewing is now a burgeoning business, many books are available at shops and libraries. Some department stores feature wine-making kits that include instructions, gadgets, and even Internal Revenue Service forms, should you be making more than 200 gallons or be planning to sell your product. Beach plums may not be mentioned in these books or kits, but if you have made a test batch of Windjammer Wine, you should know enough to adapt the methods to your own purpose.

10 *cups whole beach plums*
1 *gallon water*
2⅔ *cups sugar*
1½ *teaspoons ginger*
3 *whole cloves*
½ *envelope or ½ cake yeast*

1. Place the beach plums in a clean glass or polyethylene container. (Do not use metal or enamel containers in wine making. Toxic chemical reactions may occur.)

2. Boil the water for 5 minutes. Pour the boiling water over the beach plums. Cover the container with clean all-purpose cloth (such as Handi-Wipes) or with cheesecloth. Let the combination stand for 3 days.

3. Strain the juice through clean all-purpose cloth or cheesecloth, placed in a clean polyethylene funnel, into a clean 1-gallon glass wine jug. Wring the beach plums in the cloth, a small batch at a time, to obtain the maximum amount of juice.

4. Pour about 2 cups of the juice into a clean flameproof glass or other nonmetal saucepan. Add the sugar, ginger, and cloves. Simmer the mixture for 30 minutes, or until the sugar has dissolved and the spice flavors have infused. Pour the hot mixture into the juice in the jug.

5. When the juice in the jug is warm, but no longer hot, add the yeast. Plug the top of the jug with a ball of sterile cotton or aquarium filter floss.

6. Put the jug in a place where it will remain at 60 to 70°. Let the juice ferment for about 2 weeks. (Bubbles rising up and ringing the top of the juice indicate that fermen-

tation is occurring. Fermentation has ceased when the bubbles are no longer present.)

7. When fermentation has ceased, siphon the wine into sterile bottles, filling each bottle to the top and covering it tightly. Leave the dregs in the jug. (Screw-top soda bottles are ideal containers. Plastic tubing from an aquarium supply shop makes a good siphon.)

8. Let the wine age in a cool place for at least 3 months. Placing the bottles on a stone floor will minimize the effect of temperature changes on the wine. The longer the wine stands, the better. Try opening one bottle after 3 months, and saving the others for later in the year.

Makes about 1 gallon.

A Note on Substitutes

If you run out of beach plums but still want to prepare these recipes, you can often use substitutes. They are not nearly as good as the real thing, and I warn you that the taste of beach plums will haunt you. Nevertheless, I confess to using substitutes myself—usually in the spring when my supply is dwindling—just because I enjoy the recipes so much. A list of the best substitutes for the basic beach plum products follows. Choose the one that seems most appropriate for the recipe you are preparing and, if necessary, reduce the required amount of sugar according to your taste.

Whole and Pitted Beach Plums	Sour Cherries*
	Italian or other tart plums*
	Juniper berries†
Beach Plum Pulp	Sour cherry pulp*
	Italian or other tart plum pulp*

* Use fresh or unsweetened frozen fruit.

† Available at gourmet spice counters. Use 25 juniper berries for each cup of beach plums required.

Beach Plum Stew	Sour cherry preserves Damson or other tart plum preserves
Beach Plum Jelly	Red currant jelly Sour cherry jelly Damson or other tart plum jelly

Beach Plum Sweet-
meats and Candies
	The fruit from
	   strained sour
	   cherry, damson, or
	   other tart plum
	   preserves
	Sour cherries rolled
	   in sugar*
	Italian or other tart
	   plum pieces rolled
	   in sugar*
	Muscat or golden
	   seedless raisins

Beach Plum Shrub	A mixture of
	   grenadine syrup,
	   sugar, and cider
	   vinegar†
	Sweetened,
	   reconstituted lime
	   juice (such as
	   Rose's)

* Use ¼ cup of sugar for each cup of fruit.

† Mix ⅔ cup syrup, ¼ cup sugar, and ½ cup vinegar. Bring to a boil. Reduce the heat and simmer for 15 minutes.

A List of Recipes by Basic Beach Plum Products

Whole Beach Plums

Old Town Herring
Tidbits
Salmon Maritima
Old Maine
Lobster Stew
Anchor Duckling
Potted Beef
Buchwald
Canaan Lamb

Von Wangenheim
Veal
Gloucester Grog
Lighthouse Tea
Velours, a Beach
Plum Liqueur
Plum Crazy Brandy
Windjammer Wine

Pitted Beach Plums

Alphabet Baked
Clams
Angler's Prize
Harvest Stuffing
Ham Uncatena
Spiced Squash

Beach Plum Jam
Grand Portage
Chutney
Coastline Kuchen
Sunset Applesauce

Beach Plum Pulp

Barnacle Soup
Orient Point Chicken
Fire Island Curry
Channel Sauce

Beach Plum Butter
Plum Delicious
Sherbet

Beach Plum Stew

Plum Island
  Roast Pork
Sweet Potato Parfait
Marblehead Carrots
Mozart Omelette

Sugar Plum Drops
Sand Bars
Proselyte Cake
Humphry Marshall
  Pie

Beach Plum Jelly

Cape Cocktail
Nantucket Nuggets
Solstice Soup
Viking Soup
Sailor's Chicken
Zodiac Chicken
Red Riding Hood
  Lamb
Beach Plum Bones

Mystic Peas
Bay Sauce
Delaware Sauce
Mermaid Sauce
Beach Plum Syrup
Schubert Omelette
Fruit Foam
Syllabub
Vineyard Tea

Beach Plum Sweetmeats

Good Morning
  Muffins
Spinnakers

Post House
  Coffee Cakes
Blushing Betsys
Pilgrim Pudding

Beach Plum Candies

Veal Morsels
Bonus Cabbage

Absolutely Nuts!

Beach Plum Shrub

Block Island Broth   Plumlet
Port City Shrimp   Beach Plum Switchel
Dune Buggy

PART FIVE

THE PASTIMES
Including
Crafts and Concoctions

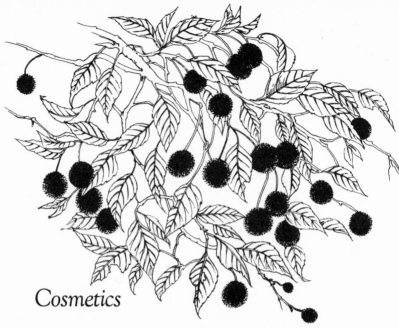

Cosmetics

GIVE YOUR SKIN A VACATION FROM COMMERCIAL PREPARA-
tions. Try the new Plum Line cosmetics. The pure ingredients bring out the best of natural beauty. The easy
treatments conjure up the carefree days of summer. While
Plum Line cosmetics are not intended to compete with
luxury treatments, the simple preparations are fun to make
and effective to use. Since inventing them, I apply them
regularly as alternatives to expensive retail products.

BLUSH OF SUMMER SKIN CONDITIONER

The most important preparation in the Plum Line,
Blush of Summer Skin Conditioner, is a luscious pink
face cream with mild astringent properties. Apply it with
the fingertips—just a bit at a time—and massage it gently
into the skin. It restores a fresh, ocean-moist feeling.

8 *whole beach plums*
2 *tablespoons white vinegar*
1 *tablespoon white petroleum jelly*
½ *teaspoon almond extract*
2 *tablespoons potato starch,*
   approximately

1. Place the beach plums in a small container with a cover, and, after they have thawed, crush them with a pestle or a potato masher. Add the vinegar. Cover the container and let the combination stand overnight.

2. Strain the liquid through all-purpose cloth (such as Handi-Wipes) or through cheesecloth into a small jar. Wring the fruit in the cloth to obtain the maximum amount of liquid. The juice will be pink. (This is because beach plum pigment, a good indicator of pH, turns pinkish when mixed with acid substances such as vinegar. It turns bluish when mixed with alkaline substances such as egg yolks.)

3. Add the petroleum jelly, the almond extract, and the potato starch to the liquid, stirring hard until the ingredients are combined. Add more potato starch if necessary to obtain the consistency of a rich, heavy cream. The potato starch acts as an emulsifier and causes the petroleum jelly to blend with the liquid. (Do not try to substitute cornstarch for potato starch; it will leave a chalky residue on your skin.)

4. Keep, covered, in the refrigerator, to retain color and consistency.

Makes about ½ cup.

BLESSING OF THE SEA SKIN TONIC

Remember the ocean spray in your face? The zing, the tingle? Capture it again with Blessing of the Sea Skin Tonic.

> ½ *cup beach plum pulp*
> ⅔ *cup water*
> ⅛ *teaspoon salt*

1. Place the ingredients in a small bowl and mix them well. Strain into a bottle. Pat Blessing of the Sea Skin Tonic on your face with your hands or with cotton. After a few minutes, rinse with lukewarm water and pat dry.
2. Keep, covered, in the refrigerator.

Makes about 1 cup.

FOURTH OF JULY FACIAL

Restore the softness of young summer days to your skin with a Fourth of July Facial. Feel it draw fatigue from your face. Boom! You're alive again.

> 1 *tablespoon beach plum pulp*
> 1 *egg white*
> 1 *teaspoon honey*

1. Place the ingredients in a small container and mix them well. Dab the facial onto your face and neck with a shaving brush or cotton ball. Leave for 10 minutes, or until your skin feels tight. Rinse with warm water and pat dry.
2. Stored in the refrigerator, the facial will keep for about one week. Stored in the freezer, it will keep indefinitely.

Makes about ⅓ cup.

SAND DUNE SPECIAL TOOTH POLISH

Get the grit off your grinders. Get the stale taste of old food out of your mouth. Use the natural refresher, Sand Dune Special Tooth Polish.

> 2 *tablespoons beach plum pulp*
> 2 *tablespoons baking soda*
> 2 *teaspoons salt*

1. Place the ingredients in a small jar and mix them well. The preparation will foam and darken.

2. Let the preparation dry for 2 days, or until it returns to the consistency of powder. Crush the powder with a spoon if it is lumpy.

3. Scoop up the polish with a wet toothbrush. Brush and rinse as usual. (Baking soda and salt are well-known tooth polishing agents, but they do not taste especially good. The addition of beach plum pulp gives the powder a refreshing taste and adds a pleasing color.)

Makes about ¼ cup.

Dyeing Wool

TRY MAKING A POT OF BEACH PLUM DYE AND DIPPING A small skein of wool. If you have never worked with natural dyes,* you will marvel at the warm, full hue you will obtain. The final color will depend on the characteristics of your particular batch of beach plums and the way you have prepared your wool. Working with very red fruit and an elementary preparation, I developed a rich, medium-pink shade.

The beach plum wool can be used for stitchery, needlepoint, rug hooking, and knitting. You can, if you get carried away, design a beach plum motif and work it all out with natural dyes.

The dyeing process is not complicated. It involves just two steps and requires only that you use plain white 100 percent wool. Other natural fibers and synthetics do not take natural dyes well.

---

* Natural dyes were once the only source of color for cloth. Their early history is linked to that of spices. The Europeans had just a few rather nondescript dyes until the Renaissance when trading vessels brought the dramatic blues, reds, and oranges from India and the Orient. Then, in 1856, an Englishman made a lavender dye from an otherwise useless coal tar ingredient. The Germans took up the process. By the turn of the century, the natural dye industry had collapsed. The use of natural dyes is being revived today, however, as interest in totally handcrafted articles is rising. Consult the bibliography for more information on this craft.

Step One—Mordanting

Mordanting means treating the wool to take and hold the dye. Mordants are chemicals of the metallic salt family that bite into the wool and ready it for the dyeing process. They also develop color. The same wool prepared with different mordants will come out of the dye pot in different colors. Powdered alum and cream of tartar, the mordant combination used in this recipe, can be found on the spice counters of many supermarkets and in drugstores. This mordant prepares the wool for beach plum as well as other types of natural dyes.

> 1 *tablespoon powdered alum*
> 1 *teaspoon cream of tartar*
> 4 *cups water*
> 1 *2-ounce skein of plain white,*
>   *100 percent wool*

1. Place the alum, cream of tartar, and water in a large enamel or stainless steel saucepan and mix them well. Heat the mordant to just below boiling, and keep it at that temperature.

2. Divide the wool into small, loose bundles so that the mordant, and later the dye, will penetrate all the strands equally. Soak the wool in the mordant for 1 hour. It is then ready for the dye pot.

Step Two—Dyeing

Prepare the dye while the wool is soaking in the mordant.

2 *cups whole beach plums*
4 *cups water*

1. Place the beach plums and water in a large enamel or stainless steel saucepan. Simmer for 1 hour, or until the fruit has colored the water. Strain the liquid through all-purpose cloth (such as Handi-Wipes) or through cheesecloth, wringing the beach plums in the cloth to obtain the maximum amount of dye. Return the dye to the saucepan.

2. Immerse the mordanted wool in the dye bath. Keeping the wool covered with dye, and keeping the dye bath hot, but not boiling, soak the wool for 1 hour. Rinse the dyed wool in cool water, and hang it up to dry. It should be colorfast after a week's airing.

3. Use more beach plums in the dye to produce a more intense color. Add rusty nails or iron pills (be sure to wash the coating off the pills) to make the dye mauve.

Growing Your Own

GROWING YOUR OWN BEACH PLUMS IMPROVES THE EN-
vironment as well as the looks of your garden. The plant,
known for its profusion of white blossoms, has a vast
root system that grabs the soil and helps hold the land
together. It does an unparalleled job of preventing ero-
sion in cliff, dune, and windswept areas. Since the plant
withstands salt, it is also recommended for roadside land-
scaping.

Beach plums will grow inland, as well as near the shore.
Planted in well-drained, sandy soil, they should thrive
on neglect, much as they do in the wild. If you want
beach plums for your garden, do not attempt to pull

them up from the dunes. Not only will your digging destroy their natural environment, but your plants will not grow. The taproot is so long—and so successful—that it can never be adequately disengaged from the soil. Go instead to a reliable nursery in beach plum territory and ask for one of the several named varieties available. Remember to buy two plants, since a single beach plum cannot fertilize itself and will not bear fruit.

Even the most inexperienced gardener, however, can grow new beach plum plants from existing ones. One simple method* involves creating suckers, a process that often occurs naturally with beach plums and other plants, such as forsythias and azaleas.

Plants From Branches

Bend a low-growing supple beach plum branch to the ground. Dig a shallow trough—about 4 inches deep and 4 inches long—where the middle part of the branch touches the sandy soil. Place the middle part of the branch in the trough, cover it with soil, and weight it down with a stone. Clip the tip of the branch to encourage the growth of roots. Roots should develop from the buried part in a year. In about two years the new plant can be severed from the parent and transplanted.

The skilled gardener may wish to try other methods of propagating beach plums. The directions follow.

* The methods were supplied by Alfred Fordham, propagator for the Arnold Arboretum of Harvard University, Jamaica Plain, Massachusetts.

Root Cuttings

Dig down around the roots of an established beach plum plant. Clip 3- or 4-inch sections from roots that are the thickness of a pencil. Place the cuttings vertically in pots of sandy soil, making sure that the up-end of the root is just two inches below the top of the soil. The plant should begin to grow in about a month and should be ready for transplanting in about a year. The best time to take root cuttings is in March or November when the plants are dormant.

Softwood Cuttings

Take 3- or 4-inch cuttings from young growth at the base of the beach plum plant. Treat them with a root-inducing substance (such as Hormodin-3) and place them under a polyethylene sheet. When the roots have developed, after about six weeks, plant the cuttings in sandy soil. Softwood cuttings should be taken at the end of June or the beginning of July, shortly after blossoming time.

Germination of Seeds

Crack the beach plum pits to obtain the seeds. (This is not easy to do. A wooden mallet works best, but an ordinary nutcracker is also effective.) Pack the seeds in moist sand or peat moss and store them at 40° for 2 or 3 months. This step shortens the time required for germination. Then plant the seeds in sandy soil. Good-sized plants should grow in about a year.

The Crop

You can anticipate a light beach plum crop about 6 years after you begin propagation. The yield should increase as the plant grows older.

Carving Wood

BEACH PLUM WOOD IS VERY HARD, BEAUTIFULLY GRAINED, and takes a fine polish. Like other kinds of plum wood, it is an excellent medium for carving. While many beach plum branches are spindly, a few, usually from older plants, are suitable for miniature works. Decorative figures, birds, and fruits, as well as useful chains, spoons, and knobs, can be carved successfully from small pieces of beach plum wood.

You should not be hurting the beach plum plant if you cut small pieces from it. Beach plums, and fruit trees in general, benefit from pruning. The best time to do the cutting is in late winter or early spring, at the end of the plant's dormant period.

Keep your pieces of fresh, green wood wrapped in damp toweling and encased in a plastic bag until you are ready to work, and while you are doing the rough carving. If the wood dries, it will split and warp. After you have completed the rough carving, treat the wood with a chemical preservative so that it will dry without being damaged. Then you can complete the fine carving.

The best preservative for green wood is polyethylene glycol-1000. Known familiarly as PEG, polyethylene glycol-1000 is a white, nontoxic chemical that looks like paraffin.* PEG works by entering the wood fibers, plugging them up with a waxlike substance, and preventing the dry wood from shrinking.

To treat your small beach plum wood carving, break about 1 pound of PEG off from the larger block of the material with an ice pick or other strong, sharp instrument. (You can estimate the correct weight from the size of your original block of PEG. For example, a 4-pound block should be broken into quarters.) Place the PEG in a plastic container, such as a wastebasket. Add 2 quarts of hot water.

After the PEG has dissolved, immerse the carving in the solution. (The solution will be about 50 percent PEG and 50 percent water by weight.) Cover the container with a plastic bag and keep the carving in the solution for about 2 weeks at room temperature. Remove the carving and let it dry for about 7 days at room tempera-

* Polyethylene glycol-1000 is available in small quantities from Crane Creek Company, P.O. Box 5553, Madison, Wisconsin, and in large quantities from Union Carbide, 6707 Whiteside Road, Baltimore, Maryland.

ture. Complete the detailed work after the carving has dried.

Varnish or oil the carving with a finish developed for use on chemically preserved wood. After this treatment, your carving should be able to withstand either constant humidity or changing weather conditions without being damaged.

Ikebana, The Art of Japanese Flower Arrangement

IF YOU CANNOT BEAR TO LEAVE THE LACY BEACH PLUM blossoms on the dunes, bring a few branches indoors to brighten your spring days. The lines are not suited to

American full-bowl designs, but they lend themselves well to Japanese arrangements.

It is not possible to present a complete manual of Ikebana here, but let me give you a few of the basic concepts and techniques. They should enable you to make some unusual beach plum blossom arrangements and to gain a great deal of quiet satisfaction in the process.*

The basic idea behind Japanese flower arrangements— and Japanese artistic creations in general—is to capture nature and hold it still for a moment in time. The rules of flower arrangement flow from this concept.

The first requirement is to have a healthy arrangement. The flowers should live as long in your bowl as they would outside. So carry a bucket of water with you when you do your cutting, and keep the ends of the branches immersed in the water. When trimming branches for your arrangement, make the cuts underwater and place the branches in the bowl immediately.

The second requirement is to keep the arrangement simple. Use just a few shapely branches. Think about what a beach plum is and what a beach plum suggests to you. Try to communicate this in your design.

The third requirement is to make the arrangement asymmetrical. This involves using an uneven number of branches (the Japanese are as superstitious about even numbers as Americans are about the number 13), positioning the branches at oblique angles, and placing the entire arrangement to one side of the bowl.

* This is a simplified, and perhaps rather unorthodox, guide to Japanese flower arrangement. Consult the bibliography for more detailed and conventional guides to this art.

To make a beach plum arrangement, you need these materials:

> **3** *shapely beach plum branches of*
> *unequal length*
> *a "frog" or spike support*
> *a shallow bowl*
> *sharp clippers*
> *a straw mat, or wooden tray, and*
> *stones (optional)*

1. Trim the small twigs from the branches to reveal the main lines. Cut each stem at an angle so that the branch will be able to absorb more water.

2. Place the first and longest branch in a not-quite-perpendicular position. Place the second, the next longest, at about a 45° angle on the other side of the imaginary perpendicular from the first. Place the third, the shortest branch, just above the horizontal on the same side of the imaginary perpendicular as the longest branch. Try to arrange the branches so that their tips all point to the center of the design. (See the illustration on page 132 for an example.)

3. Then, if you wish, place the entire arrangement on a mat or tray that suggests the sea, and add some stones to suggest the dunes. This gives you a small world in a bowl.

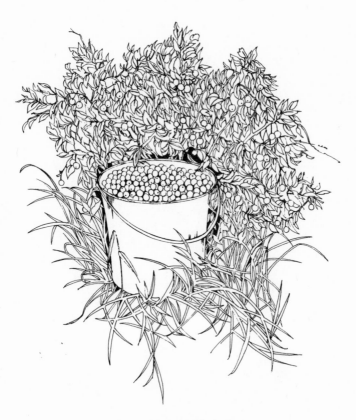

BIBLIOGRAPHY
and
INDEX

Bibliography

ADROSKO, RITA J. *Natural Dyes and Home Dyeing.* New York: Dover, 1971.

American Heritage Cookbook. Edited by the editors of American Heritage. New York: American Heritage Publishing Co., 1964.

BAILEY, JOHN S., AND TOMLINSON, WILLIAM E. *The Beach Plum in Massachusetts.* University of Massachusetts Extension Publication 315, Reprinted September 1961.

BAILEY, LIBERTY H. *The Standard Cyclopedia of Horticulture.* New York: The Macmillan Co., 1937.

BRERETON, JOHN. *A Briefe and True Relation of the Discoverie of the Northern Part of Virginia.* Facsimile of the 1602 edition. New York: Dodd Mead and Co., 1903.

Cape Cod Beach Plum Growers Association Circular 4 (mimeo), 1952.

CARR, RACHEL E. *The Japanese Way With Flowers.* New York: Harper & Row, 1965.

"Chappy-Born Beach Plum Bushes are Now Assured a Place in the Hall of Fame," *Vineyard Gazette* (Martha's Vineyard, Mass.), March 8, 1957.

COE, STELLA. *The Art of Japanese Flower Arangement.* New York: John Day Co., 1966.

Composition of Foods. U.S. Department of Agriculture Handbook 8. Washington, D.C.: U.S. Government Printing Office, 1963.

COON, NELSON. *Using Wayside Plants.* Rev. Ed. New York: Hearthside Press, 1969.

Curtis's Botanical Magazine, Illustrating and Describing the Plants of the Royal Botanic Gardens of Kew. Vol. 5. D. Prain, Ed., London: Lovell Reeve and Co., 1909.

DAVIS, S. G., AND LEVINE, A. S. "Composition and Utilization of the Beach Plum." *The Fruit Products Journal* 21, (August 1942): 361–364.

"Directions for the Treatment of Cross Sections of Green

Logs and Limbwood to Prevent Splitting and Checking," Forest Products Laboratory of the U.S. Department of Agriculture (mimeo), Madison, Wis., 1970.

FLYNN, EMILY C. "Make Your Own Dyes from Plants," *Horticulture* 31 (September 1971): 43–45.

GIBBONS, EUELL. *Stalking the Blue-Eyed Scallop.* New York: David McKay Co., 1964.

GRAVES, GEORGE. "The Beach Plum, Its Written Record." Reprinted from *The National Horticulture Magazine*, April 1944, pp. 73–97.

JONES, FRANK H., AND SNOW, INA S. Cape Cod Beach Plum Growers Bulletin 10 (mimeo), April 1958.

KEYS, A., GRANDE, F., AND ANDERSON, J. T. "Fiber and Pectin in the Diet and Serum Cholesterol Concentration in Man," *Proceedings of the Society for Experimental Biology and Medicine* 106 (March 1961): 555–558.

KING, LOUISE TATE, AND WEXLER, JEAN STEWART. *The Martha's Vineyard Cookbook.* New York: Harper and Row, 1971.

KOROTKOV, I. L. "Vitamin C Content of Black Currants." *Voprosy Pitaniia* 20 (July–August 1969): 71–72.

Larousse Gastronomique. Compiled by Prosper Montagné. New York: Crown Publishers, 1961.

LIVSHITS, D. D. "Preventative Role of Local Pectin-Containing Food Products in Lead Poisonings." *Voprosy Pitaniia* 28 (July–August 1969): 76–77.

"Looking Towards Beach Plum Cultivation," Bulletin of the Arnold Arboretum, Jamaica Plain, Mass. Vol. 9, Nos. 11-12, December 1949.

MAMCHUR, F. I., KULEVNIK, I. I., AND ZBIRAK, N. P. "Effect of Medicinal Substances from Spruces, Firs, and Wild Carrot Seeds on the Bile Forming Function of the Liver." *Vrachebnoe Delo* 6 (June 1969): 132–134.

MARSHALL, HUMPHRY. *Arbustum Americanum: The American Grove.* Facsimile of the 1785 edition. New York: Hafner, 1967.

MITCHELL, HAROLD L. "PEG is the Sweetheart of the Wood Craftsman." *Yearbook of Agriculture*, 1968, 147–149.

MITCHELL, HAROLD L., AND IVERSON, E. S. "Seasoning Green-Wood Carvings with Polyethylene Glycol-1000." *Forest Products Journal*, January 1961.

NAKEEB, M. A., EL-, AND YOUSEF, R. T. "Study of the Anti-microbial Action of Pectin" (I), and "Study of the Anti-bacterial and Antifungal Activities of Pectin" (II). *Planta Medica* 18 (May 1970): 201–209.

PETRIDES, GEORGE A. *A Field Guide to Trees and Shrubs.* Boston: Houghton Mifflin, 1958.

PHILLIPS, W. E. J., AND BRIEN, R. L. "Effect of Pectin, a Hypocholesterolemic Polysaccharide, on Vitamin A Utilization in the Rat." *Journal of Nutrition* 100 (March 1970): 289–292.

POLANSKY, M. M., AND MURPHY, E. W. "Vitamin B6 in Fruits and Nuts." *Journal of the American Dietetic Association* 48 (February 1966): 109–115.

A Report on the Trees and Shrubs Growing Naturally in the Forests of Massachusetts. Compiled by the Commissioners on the Zoological and Botanical Survey of the State. Boston: Charles C. Little and James Brown, 1850.

RITCHIE, WILLIAM A. *The Archaeology of Martha's Vineyard.* New York: Natural History Press, 1969.

RUTLEDGE, DEBORAH. *Natural Beauty Secrets.* New York: Avon, 1966.

SCHERY, ROBERT W. *How Plants Work for Man.* Englewood Cliffs, N.J.: Prentice-Hall, 1963.

STERLING, DOROTHY. *The Outer Lands.* New York: Natural History Press, 1967.

TROIAN, A. V., AND BORUKH, I. F. "Carpathian Wild Berries as a Source of Mineral Substances." *Voprosy Pitaniia* 24 (March–April 1965): 84–85.

WANGENHEIM, F. A. J. VON. *Beschreibung einiger Nordamericanischen Holz- und Buscharten.* Göttingen: J. C. Dieterich, 1781.

———. *Beytrag zur teutschen holzgerechten Forstwissenschaft, die Ampflanzung Nordamericanischer Holzarten.* Göttingen: J. C. Dieterich, 1787.

WAUGH, FRANK A. *Plums and Plum Culture*. New York: Orange Judd Publishing Co., 1901.

WELLS, A. F., AND ERSHOFF, B. H. "Beneficial Effects of Pectin in Prevention of Hypercholesterolemia and Increase in Liver Cholesterol in Cholesterol-Fed Rats." *Journal of Nutrition* 74 (1961): 87–92.

WIGHT, WILLIAM F. *Native American Species of Prunus*. U.S. Department of Agriculture Bulletin 179. Washington, D.C.: U.S. Government Printing Office, 1915.

ZOOK, E. G., AND LEHMANN, J. "Mineral Composition of Fruits" (I and II). *Journal of the American Dietetic Association* 52 (March 1968): 218–231.

Index